GO WEST YOUNG MAN!

GO WEST

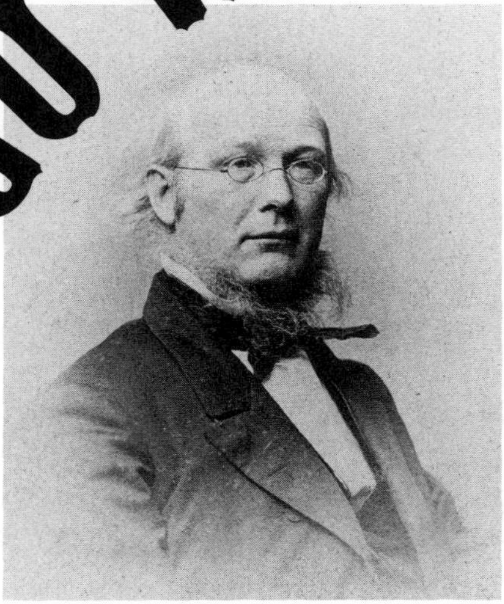

YOUNG MAN!

HORACE

GREELEY'S

COY F. CROSS II

VISION FOR

UNIVERSITY OF NEW MEXICO PRESS
ALBUQUERQUE

AMERICA

Frontispiece:
Horace Greeley, founder and editor of
New York Tribune *and advocate*
of western development.
(Courtesy University
of Rochester Library)

Library of Congress
Cataloging-in-Publication Data
Cross, Coy F.
Go west, young man!
Horace Greeley's vision for America
Coy F. Cross II. — 1st ed.
        p. cm.
Includes bibliographical
references and index.

Contents

Introduction: Greeley and the
safety valve—Editor and advocate
of the West—Educating farmers for
their noble profession—Advocating
land reform and the Homestead Act
—Battling slavery in the expanding
West —Fighting for the railroad west
—Supporting association and the
union colony—Epilogue.

ISBN 0-8263-1605-0

1. Greeley, Horace, 1811-1872
—Views on West (U.S.)
2. Land settlement—West (U.S.)
—History—19th cenury.
3. Public lands-West (U.S.)
—History—19th century.
4. West (U.S.)—History.
I. Title.
E415.9.G8C85 1995
978'.02—dc   2094-18709
                CIP

*Dedicated to
Professor Alex DeConde,
mentor and friend*

CONTENTS

PREFACE

Most people who recognize Horace Greeley's name immediately associate him with the phrase "Go West, young man."[1] Few know any more about him, even though his autobiography, *Recollections of a Busy Life,* and several biographies are readily available, including a contemporary work by James Parton[2] and Glyndon G. Van Deusen's excellent *Horace Greeley: Nineteenth-Century Crusader.*

This book is not a duplication of these earlier works. It focuses on Greeley's efforts to open the West for settlement as an answer to the problems of poverty and unemployment in New York City. Although other historians have acknowledged Greeley's belief that the West was a "safety valve"—Henry Nash Smith, in *Virgin Land: The American West as Symbol and Myth,* called him "the best known exponent of the idea"[3]—no one has investigated his efforts to use the safety-valve theory to populate the West with the urban poor. Despite more than thirty years of persuading, cajoling, and pleading, New York City's poor did not move West. Yet Greeley's work was not in vain: millions of others heeded his words, and his endeavors smoothed their path westward.

My interest in Horace Greeley and the history of the American West began in 1985 in Professor Will Jacobs's American History seminar at the University of California, Santa Barbara. I appreciate the indulgence and comments of those in Will's seminars, who undoubtedly learned more about Horace Greeley than they ever wanted to know. I would also like to thank the staffs at the Huntington Library, San Marino, California; the New York City Public Library; the University of Rochester Library; the New York Historical Society; the National Archives; the Greeley, Colorado, Municipal Museum; and the University of California, Santa Barbara. I especially want to thank my friend Professor Wilbur Jacobs, who introduced me to Greeley, revived my interest in Frederick Jackson Turner, and offered his assistance and encouragement throughout this project.

GO WEST YOUNG MAN!

INTRODUCTION
GREELEY AND THE SAFETY VALVE

Want is a hard master anywhere; but nowhere else are the sufferings, the woes, the desperation, of utter need so trying as in a great city; and they are preeminently so in this city; because the multiplicity of the destitute benumbs the heart of charity and precludes attention to any one's wants.

Horace Greeley, *Recollections*

There is a class of drinking, hunting, frolicking, rarely working, frontiersmen, who seem to have been created on purpose to erect log cabins and break paths in advance of a different class of settlers who regularly come in to push them out and start them along after a few years.

Horace Greeley, *What I Know of Farming*

3

More than fifty years before Frederick Jackson Turner presented his paper on "The Significance of the Frontier in American History" and more than sixty years before he explained how the West was the nation's "safety valve," drawing off the discontented workers and excess population in the East, Horace Greeley had accepted that premise as truth.[1] Greeley, the owner and editor of the *New York Tribune*, America's leading newspaper of the day, spent the next thirty-five years working to open the West as a haven for his city's poor. Greeley did not originate the idea but, as Henry Nash Smith said, he was its best-known proponent in the mid-nineteenth century.

In August 1831, twenty-year-old Horace Greeley arrived in New York City with his worldly possessions wrapped in a handkerchief, ten dollars in his pocket, and a deep faith in the conservative American virtues of hard work and frugality. This faith seemed justified: within three years he and a partner had founded a profitable printing business and were publishing the *New Yorker*, a weekly magazine devoted to America's budding literature with political commentary. By 1836 Greeley had accumulated a personal estate worth five thousand dollars and had an annual income of about one thousand dollars, sufficient to support himself and a wife.

Unfortunately for Greeley, the American economy of the 1830s was a house of cards. Near the end of 1836, a wave of bankruptcies affected nearly everyone, especially merchants and bankers, and plunged the country into the worst depres-

4   *Introduction*

sion of its first century. By the end of the decline in 1843, prices had fallen to half their previous levels and unemployment in the industrial sections of the country topped 20 percent. New York City was among the hardest hit.

Greeley's financial fortunes paralleled those of his city. Subscribers to the *New Yorker* dropped from nine thousand to six thousand within a few months, and those who continued to subscribe seldom paid. He and his partner split their assets, the partner taking the printing business and its small profit and Greeley keeping the *New Yorker*. He borrowed from friends and professional lenders to meet expenses he could no longer postpone. His debt quickly became so onerous that he offered to pay anyone two thousand dollars to take the magazine's assets and assume its obligations. He later lamented the "horrors of bankruptcy" and discouraged borrowing or indebtedness.[2]

Despite his financial woes, the "filth, squalor, rags, dissipation, want, and misery" of his neighbors made a deep and lasting impression on Greeley and other reform-minded Americans.[3] He began to doubt the age-old wisdom that poverty resulted from a lack of industry and was somehow a blessing in disguise. Even some "new-thought" religious groups, such as the Universalists and Greeley's Unitarians, had begun to abandon "the poor will always be with us" for an ideology based on "the perfectibility of man."[4] Wanting to help, but having little money, Greeley served on community committees that solicited funds and visited the poor. He saw the extreme conditions firsthand and later recalled the suffering of those he visited, including two large families who lived in a cellar under a stable, "a prey to famine on the one hand, and to vermin and cutaneous maladies on the other, with sickness adding its horrors to those of a polluted atmosphere and a wintry temperature."[5]

Horace Greeley, editor, reformer, and political ally of William Seward and Thurlow Weed. (Courtesy University of Rochester Library)

As the depression, with its accompanying despair and hunger, stretched into years, the compassionate editor began to seek a universal answer for the suffering of the urban poor. In the winter of 1839–40, he wrote a series of articles asking, "What shall be done for the Laborer?" As he searched for answers to this question, Greeley fondly recalled the farm of his youth and began to consider the benefits of city dwellers migrating to the countryside. He first suggested that the poor move to the farming region surrounding New York City, but soon realized there were too few acres to accommodate them. It was then that he expanded his vision, telling the poor to "Go West!"

The virtues of country life and the value of the West as a sanctuary for the East's discontented masses were not new ideas. For centuries city-dwelling intellectuals had proclaimed the nobility of the country and lamented the depravity of the cities.[6] Thomas Jefferson believed that the size of the American continent would allow its citizens to develop a nation of independent farms instead of recreating the squalor-filled cities that dominated Europe. Ralph Waldo Emerson, Greeley's contemporary, admired the country, which, he believed, created self-directed, gifted, and virtuous men, and condemned the cities filled with "a supple, glib-tongued tribe, who live for show, servile to public opinion." Henry David Thoreau, for whom Greeley acted as literary agent, advocated abandoning the cities and towns and withdrawing into the wilderness. Thoreau said, "I must walk toward Oregon and not toward Europe."[7]

Historian Ray Allen Billington, Turner's successor as the champion of the frontier thesis, found that even the leaders of the Massachusetts Bay Colony believed that the West would draw off the East's discontented poor. Governor John Winthrop recommended limiting poor colonists' land holdings to prevent them from abandoning their work in the townships for opportunity on the edges of "civilization." Billington quoted Benjamin Franklin, George Washington, Thomas Jefferson, and Alexander Hamilton, among others, to prove that they, too, viewed the West as a refuge for the oppressed. By the nineteenth century, he said, the safety-valve theory had such widespread acceptance that it was part of the American creed.[8]

While Greeley sought a solution for all urban workers and their families, most contemporary reformers focused on smaller groups. Robert M. Hartley, for example, organized the Association for Improving the Condition of the Poor (AICP) in 1843. He crusaded to outlaw milk from cows fed from distillery refuse, claiming it was unfit and contributed to a rising infant mortality rate. The AICP also organized New York City's thirty to forty charitable societies so that their coordinated efforts could more efficiently serve the needs of the city's poor. Although Hartley and the AICP helped to improve general living conditions in New York, their efforts concentrated on individual families.[9] Another reformer, Charles Loring Brace, like Greeley, saw the West as a home for New York's poor. But Brace concentrated on helping the thousands of orphaned or abandoned children who lived on the city's streets. In 1853 he organized the Children's Aid Society to find foster homes in rural areas for New York City's vagrant children. By 1873 the society had moved nearly twenty thousand youngsters from the city streets to rural homes both nearby and farther west. Although many of them had difficulty adjusting to their new life, subsequent studies concluded that most adapted and the results were "amazingly successful."[10]

Greeley, on the other hand, saw the West as the ideal home for New York City's unemployed workers and their families, people who were willing and able to work if only they had the opportunity. Although the exact location of "the West" moved as Greeley's perception of opportunity and politics changed, he believed that some people would do well anywhere, if they only had a fair chance. Others, he argued, would be beggars if they and a thousand like them had California all to themselves.[11] He used the pages of the *Tribune* to attract the attention of the people he thought should emigrate. As motivation, he painted a glowing picture of opportunity, writing of the fertile lands in the West, where a hardworking couple could build their own farm within a few years. He encouraged people to go west to find better lives for themselves, to relieve the poverty in eastern cities, to populate "unsettled" western areas, and to strengthen the United States economically and politically.

After deciding that peopling the West with New York City's poor, unemployed workers would not only relieve the suffering of the masses but also would strengthen the country by populating its midsection (assuming, like Turner, that it was unoccupied), Greeley devoted himself to making this vision a reality. His cry, "Go West, young man," began in 1837 and continued for the rest of his life. Although his goal of helping the eastern poor resettle on western farms remained constant, the location of Greeley's West (like Turner's) was difficult to locate or define. For Greeley the optimum site for settlement often changed to reflect his politics or his thoughts on what was best for the nation as a whole.

Throughout most of the 1840s, Greeley's West lay in what is today America's Midwest. In 1842 he lauded Wisconsin for its mineral wealth, rich soil, and amiable climate. He believed it was destined to become a prosperous farming region. When a Wisconsin editor later criticized Greeley for being hostile to any western settlement, he responded that he had done more to extol the virtues of Wisconsin than any other editor east of Buffalo. He described his ideal spot for relocating as "this side of the jumping-off place," where affordable land had already been surveyed.[12]

Illinois was another of Greeley's perennial favorites. During an 1847 visit he considered the region's fertility and productive capacity to be beyond description. More than a decade later he still considered Illinois to have the best soil he had ever seen.[13] After noting there was still plenty of good land available there, Greeley predicted that within the lifetime of children then living, Illinois' population would surpass ten million and Chicago's more than one million.[14] He was only half right. Chicago reached a population of one million in 1890; however, the state did not exceed ten million until 1960.

This friend of western migration saw promise in almost any part of the Midwest, from Buffalo and Pittsburgh in the East to St. Paul and Independence, Missouri, in the West. Greeley encouraged emigrants to move to the fertile states of Illinois, Iowa, and Wisconsin, instead of lingering in New York, where they could barely survive.[15] Although Minnesota had a cold climate with long and severe winters, he considered it an ideal location, with fertile soil and abundant timber and water. Indiana was not quite as fertile as Illinois but had more timber. Iowa did not match Illinois' fertility either, but its timber was more widespread and there was more water available. He also described Kansas as fertile and well watered, but saved his highest praise for Missouri, where only the presence of slavery and the absence of schools prevented it from being the "most inviting State for emigrants in the Union."[16]

Other factors besides the best land at the best price influenced the locations he recommended. After William Henry Harrison's death in 1841 and John Tyler's ascendancy to the presidency, the dispute between the United States and Great Britain over the Oregon Territory rekindled. Rallying to Tyler's slogan, "Fifty-four Forty or Fight," many Americans were ready to go to war for that remote section of the continent. Others hoped to improve America's claim and their own fortune by moving there. Greeley opposed both the fight and the flight to the Northwest.

In February 1843 Greeley explained his opposition to Oregon. The national treasury was already "destitute of funds," and extending the protection and services of the federal government to such a remote area would be expensive. He also

Introduction

doubted that Oregon was worth a war with Great Britain.[17] Furthermore, like many others of his day, he believed that democracy had geographic limitations. The great distance and two mountain ranges would separate Oregon's federal representatives from their constituents; therefore, the voters would have no control over their elected officials. The distance also would prevent Oregon from developing the common interests and close ties with the rest of the country that Greeley considered essential to democratic government.[18]

In 1845 he expressed the same reservations about California.[19] Expanding to the West Coast would overextend the nation's democratic institutions, causing them to collapse. A few years later, after Oregon and California had become states, Greeley used the same reasoning to justify a transcontinental railroad. The undertaking was necessary to overcome the distance and the natural barriers that separated the country's citizens from their federal government.[20]

While California belonged to Mexico, Greeley discouraged migration there—calling the Great Plains and the mountain ranges an excellent national boundary. But after the Mexican War had won this prize for the United States, he changed his mind. Calling California the "young Queen of the Pacific," he predicted that its trade and commercial influence would soon rival New York's.[21] After he visited the "young queen" in 1859, he asserted that no other state could compare. In 1868 he equated the discovery of gold in California so soon after the area became American territory with the most memorable and fortunate events in the history of humankind.[22]

Following the Civil War, Greeley's West moved south. Having written such scathing condemnations of the southern firebrands in the years before the war, he used his persuasive abilities and personal influence to help heal the wounds after the fighting was over. (Greeley even signed the bond that freed Jefferson Davis from his northern prison.) The editor suggested that people with money to invest could find inexpensive land with "tillage, timber and buildings" in the South.[23] In 1870 he noted that Virginia, the Carolinas, and Georgia were encouraging immigrants as they never had before.[24]

But whether this West was in western New York, in the nation's midsection, or in California, it had certain characteristics the immigrant should look for. In an 1842 editorial, Greeley counseled "mechanics" (a generic term for skilled workers, such as carpenters) to move with their families to an area with good soil and water, a healthful climate, a supply of timber, inexpensive land, and with prospects for quickly increasing in population and in wealth. The location should not be too remote, but near enough to settled areas to have schools, roads, mills, good markets, and a steady demand for labor. One could generally find such locations in newly established towns or in regions of recent or planned internal improvements. Turner would later call these places "the frontier."[25] Greeley advised settlers not to move past the "bounds of civilization," but to "stop this side of the end of the woods," where they would have access to schools, mail service, and a doctor for emergencies.[26]

While expounding on the who, the why, and the where, Horace Greeley labored to provide the how. While he used his literary and persuasive gifts to sell the notion of going West to his many readers, he worked to open the West through better agriculture, free land, a transcontinental railroad, and slave-free territories. "Go West! young man!" was neither a simple response to a question nor a campaign slogan—it was Horace Greeley's lifelong dream and vision for the future of his country. But who was Greeley, and why was his belief in the safety-valve theory, which current scholars have disproved, important?

1

HORACE GREELEY

EDITOR AND ADVOCATE OF THE WEST

The real power of the Press in this country began with Greeley, and if it did not end with him, it has gained nothing since.

Albert E. Pillsbury,
"Memorial to Horace Greeley"

Instead of being limited to preponderant influence within a particular locality, a widely distributed constituency scattered from Maine to California, furnished the basis of a power of national scope, and at times enabled the editor to mold public sentiment more effectively than even the President.

Ralph Fahrney, Greeley biographer

13

In 1860 Horace Greeley, editor and founder of the *New York Tribune,* was one of the most influential and popular people in America. The previous year he had taken an arduous overland journey across the Great Plains to California. Although he had championed the West for more than twenty years, this was his first look at Kansas, Colorado, and California. By the time his trek had ended in October 1859, he could speak with even greater conviction when he said, "Go West, young man!"

This advocate of the West and "the real power of the Press in this country" was born on his family's eighty-acre farm near Amherst, New Hampshire, on February 3, 1811, the eldest of Zack and Mary Greeley's five children. Zack's poor management, speculation, and improvident loan to a friend, as well as the panic of 1819, led to foreclosure on the Greeley farm when Horace was eight, although years later the son attributed the loss to his parents' use of "ardent spirits" and tobacco.[1] On New Year's Day 1824, before he was thirteen, Greeley took a pledge to abstain from distilled liquor, a vow he apparently kept. The poverty and hardships of the next few years left a lasting impression on the lad, and helped him to become a compassionate man.

Young Greeley decided to become a printer and, in 1826 at age fifteen, convinced the editor of the *Northern Spectator,* in nearby East Poultney, Vermont, to employ him as an apprentice. A short time later the rest of the Greeley clan moved to Erie County, Pennsylvania. But Horace, having found his

Editor and Advocate of the West

niche, stayed in Vermont. The editor of the *Spectator* was often away and left the young apprentice on his own to do much of the work of writing and publishing the paper. The apprenticeship was a grand opportunity to not only learn the newspaper business but also read extensively on politics, and the townspeople often solicited his opinion. By the time the doors of the newspaper closed in the spring of 1830, Horace Greeley had found the profession that would fill his life and discovered the two subjects that would dominate his newspaper: politics and reform.

Greeley soon joined his family in Pennsylvania, but after a short stint as a journeyman printer at the *Erie Gazette,* he left for New York City. He arrived on August 17, 1831, with ten dollars in his pocket and his worldly goods tied up in a handkerchief. The young printer was nearly six feet tall and, at less than one hundred forty-five pounds, appeared gangly. His features were pale and delicate, almost feminine. The soft blue eyes and white hair he had as a baby still dominated his appearance, and would continue to do so for the rest of his life. After several days of walking the streets seeking work, Greeley finally secured a position setting type for a New Testament. The small type size, frequent italics, and references in Greek letters made the work so tedious and the pay so small that no one else wanted the job. He worked fourteen to sixteen hours a day just to meet his meager expenses.[2]

During the next several months Greeley found enough work to earn about six dollars a week and managed to live on half that. Near the end of 1832, he and a friend, investing their meager savings of less than two hundred dollars and stretching their credit to the limit, opened a print shop. One incentive for starting the business was the contract to print a new "cheap" newspaper for Dr. H. D. Shepard. The first issue of the *Morning Post,* edited by Shepard, reached New York's streets on January 1, 1833, and sold for two cents. However, a sudden cold wave and Dr. Shepard's lack of experience combined to create obstacles too great for the new enterprise. "Thus the first cheap-for-cash daily in New York—perhaps in the world—died when scarcely yet a month old," Greeley explained. "We printers were hard aground on a lee shore, with little prospect of getting off."[3]

The young partners were able to "refloat" their enterprise, and it slowly prospered. On March 22, 1834, they published the first edition of the *New Yorker,* a magazine mainly devoted to current literature but including election returns and political commentary.[4] The *New Yorker* and the printing business prospered sufficiently to allow Greeley to support a wife. He had met Mary Cheney, a schoolteacher, when both were living in Dr. Sylvester Graham's boardinghouse. Dr. Graham, who became world renown for his Graham cracker, advocated a rigid diet of simple foods. When Mary moved to North Carolina, Greeley soon followed her and proposed. They wed at Warrenton, North Carolina, on July 5, 1836, and returned to New York to live. Mary continued to follow Dr. Graham's diet, and she persuaded Horace to do so, which accounted for the rather unattractive "cuisine" on the Greeley's dinner table.

The editor of the *New Yorker* estimated his worth at five thousand dollars in 1836 and his annual income at about one thousand dollars, both above average for the owner of a small business. Near the end of the year, however, the Bank of England determined that the flow of hard currency to the United States was excessive and reduced the capital available for investment in the former colonies. This coincided with the demise of the United States Bank, which failed to survive Presidents Andrew Jackson and Martin Van Buren's attacks.

The immediate reduction in available credit, coupled with a concurrent decrease in the British demand for cotton, set off a wave of bankruptcies that plunged the American economy into depression.

The "Commercial Revulsion of 1837," Greeley recalled, "swept over the land, whelming it [the *New Yorker*] and me in general ruin."[5] Subscriptions fell drastically, and those who subscribed seldom paid. Greeley, faced with a loss of one hundred dollars per week, continued publishing the magazine while looking for other sources of income to keep himself and his business solvent. His own financial plight and memories of his childhood made him acutely aware of the abject poverty of New York's poor workers. Finding a solution for their condition became a lifelong goal for the reforming editor.

A new opportunity to improve his personal finances presented itself in late 1837. Thurlow Weed, the Whig boss and Albany journalist, decided to publish a political weekly to support the gubernatorial candidacy of his friend William H. Seward. Weed had never met Greeley, but he had read the *New Yorker*, and its politics and literacy impressed him. He visited Greeley in New York and offered him one thousand dollars to edit the proposed weekly for one year. Greeley quickly accepted. Thus also was born the political partnership of Weed, Seward, and Greeley, which would last until 1854.

Greeley suggested they call the new paper the *Jeffersonian* to give it a republican flavor. The first edition appeared on February 17, 1838, and circulation grew to fifteen thousand a week. The editor tried to convince his readers "by candor and moderation, rather than overbear by passion and vehemence."[6] Throughout the year, Greeley commuted weekly by riverboat between New York and Albany. On Sunday mornings he could be seen rushing down the gangplank with white coattails fly-

Thurlow Weed, New York political boss and Greeley's ally.
(Courtesy University of Rochester Library)

Editor and Advocate of the West

ing as he returned to New York from Albany. The enterprise succeeded and Seward became governor. The *Jeffersonian* ceased publication in February 1839.

Weed, in the meantime, determined to duplicate the 1838 tactic in the 1840 presidential campaign. He wanted to publish a Whig paper in support of William Henry Harrison's candidacy, and Greeley was again to be the editor. The *Log Cabin* began publication in April of 1840, amid the partisan jeers of James Gordon Bennett in the Democratic *New York Herald.* Greeley later claimed that the political weekly's circulation quickly reached eighty thousand and could have grown to more than one hundred thousand if he had had adequate facilities.[7] Again the undertaking succeeded, and Harrison, with the help of the *Log Cabin,* became president.

Greeley continued to publish the *Log Cabin* after the election, and it maintained a circulation of about ten thousand. The *New Yorker,* by then, was breaking even, and it, too, continued publication. Following the Whig success in the election of 1840, several of the party leaders encouraged Greeley to begin an inexpensive newspaper in New York. The Whig daily would appeal to the laboring class, the same audience to whom he had directed the *New Yorker.*[8] Benjamin Day's *Sun* and Bennett's *Herald* had proven that penny papers could succeed. Within the first four years of publication, the *Herald* had already surpassed the *London Times* in circulation. Whig leaders Noah Cook and James Coggeshall provided a list of five hundred subscribers, and Coggeshall lent Greeley one thousand dollars for the new paper.

With two thousand dollars of his own money and the one thousand dollars borrowed from Coggeshall, Greeley purchased the newly developed presses and other equipment that made the printing of a penny paper possible. He selected his paper's name very carefully. The *Tribune* would fight for the rights of the common people.[9] The first issue reached the streets of New York on April 10, 1841, as snow fell, the wind blew, and the city mourned the death of President Harrison. Newsboys sold the paper for one cent. Greeley printed five thousand copies and "nearly succeeded in giving away all of them that would not sell." In July, Thomas McElrath, a successful attorney who had been part owner of the publishing firm that had leased Greeley his first print shop, offered to pay the editor two thousand dollars for a full partnership in the *Tribune*. More important, McElrath would be the business manager, leaving Greeley free to devote his time to the content of the paper. For the next ten years McElrath helped create a financially successful newspaper, while Greeley pursued his "anti-Slavery, anti-Hanging, Socialist, and other frequent aberrations from the straight and narrow path of Whig partisanship."[10]

The *Tribune*'s assistant editor was Henry J. Raymond, a young man who had worked part time for the *New Yorker*. Raymond left the *Tribune* and later, in 1851, founded the *New York Times*. Although Greeley often referred to his rival as "The Little Villain," he also praised Raymond as the cleverest journalist he had ever seen.[11]

Even after the birth of the daily *Tribune*, Greeley continued to publish the *New Yorker* and the *Log Cabin*. In August 1841 he wrote his friend Rufus Griswold, soliciting a buyer for the *New Yorker*.[12] Not finding one, in September 1841 Greeley merged the literary magazine and the *Log Cabin* with the *Weekly Tribune*, a national edition of the *Tribune* providing news to readers outside of New York City. He encouraged his cash-poor readers in the rural areas to form *Tribune* clubs so they could share the cost of the subscription and discuss the ideas espoused by the editor. Soon, farmers and townsfolk

Editor and Advocate of the West

alike were gathering at the post office or around the cracker barrel at the general store to see what "Old Horace" had to say this week. The new journal, which contained the best of the daily editorials and comments, became the gospel for rural Americans, especially thousands of prairie farmers, many of whom migrated west during the 1840s and 1850s. After New York, *Tribune* readership was greatest in Pennsylvania, Ohio, Illinois, and Indiana—all critical states in national affairs. But readers in all the western states and territories subscribed, and Greeley published a special edition for California.

Known as the "Great Moral Organ," the *Tribune,* as Greeley's voice, addressed the great social issues of the mid-nineteenth century. He claimed sole responsibility for the newspaper's content. Although he did not *write* every word, his employees could attest to his habit of *reading* every word.[13] The editorials spoke out against slavery, war, rum, grog shops, tobacco, seduction, brothels, and gambling houses. Politics also filled the *Tribune*'s pages. Greeley supported what he considered to be the four great principles of Whiggery: protection, which would increase the number of producers in the country; a stable currency; internal improvements; and better lives for the masses.[14] These were the issues closest to westerners' hearts. In addition, he used his newspaper to extol the virtues of the West and the opportunities that awaited young, hardworking couples who migrated there.

Greeley's enthusiasm for the West occasionally lead him to make claims that later proved to be overly optimistic. But his *New York Tribune* was no "Booster Press," a term Historian Daniel Boorstin used to described western newspapers whose sole purpose was to create communities that would attract subscribers. By 1860 it was the most widely read newspaper in the United States, and perhaps in the world, with an estimated one million readers. Called "one of the great leaders of the nation," the *Tribune* was no upstart, but the established leader of America's mass media in the 1850s.[15] Horace Greeley used this powerful tool not in city building, but in nation building.

Greeley advocated internal improvements, but not at the cost of the environment. He sought to protect the wilderness and its wildlife. He recognized that clear cutting would destroy the soil and the streams and rivers. Stripping the timber in upstate New York would cause the Hudson River to become unnavigable for much of the year and result in devastating floods from Utica to Castleton, he warned.[16]

Greeley also used his paper as a forum for the ideas of many of the leading economists and social reformers of his day. Henry Carey's comments on protection and tariffs and excerpts from his *Harmony of Interests, Agricultural, Manufacturing and Commercial* appeared in *Tribune* editorials. Greeley published and expounded on William Atchinson's attacks on the sins of laissez-faire capitalism. Governments, the editor believed, should promote the well-being of the people by providing enough work for the individual to earn his or her subsistence; but governments should not own the means of production. Thomas Carlyle's *Past and Present* was the greatest book of the century, according to Greeley. Carlyle, a Scottish critic of social injustice, considered land to be the source of a nation's wealth. Governments, he said, could eradicate social injustice by making land available to everyone and by encouraging popular migration, a philosophy that prompted the call "Go West, young man!" Charles Fourier, a Frenchman who advocated utopian socialism, also greatly influenced Greeley. According to Fourier, people were instinctively good, but could only realize their natural goodness if society reorganized into small economic units. These units could then combine to form a joint stock company, with members investing their labor, capital, and talents.

Editor and Advocate of the West

There were still more sides to Greeley. While espousing utopian socialism on one hand, he supported fiscal constraint on
the other. Part liberal reformer, part conservative pragma-
tist, he always pursued the course he believed was best for
the country. The *Tribune,* for example, treated slavery cau-
tiously in the 1840s. Greeley considered slavery a moral evil,
but out of concern for national unity, he seldom attacked it
during the early years. When the peculiar institution began
to divide the nation and break up the Whig Party, however, it
became the focus for many of his most biting editorials.

Concern for national unity also prevented Greeley from
supporting unbridled western expansion. He, like many other
enlightened thinkers of his day, feared that the country would
outgrow the limits of democratic rule. Democracy could pre-
vail only where the voters were close enough to the center of
power to keep close watch on those in office. Greeley believed
Oregon, for example, was too far away from the nation's capital to effectively participate in the government. He felt it best
to leave Oregon under the mutual protection of the United
States and Great Britain, because to include such distant territory in the United States would be expensive and would
weaken the democracy.[17] Greeley believed that only a cohesive nation, upholding the dignity of the individual and guar-
anteeing opportunity for all, could achieve greatness.[18]

He also believed that if the nation's West was going to be
the land of opportunity, it must be free from slavery: free labor would not migrate into "slave" territories. As the controversy over the annexation of Texas and the war with Mexico
helped focus the country's attention on the extension of slavery into new territories, both Seward and Greeley became
more active in the antislavery cause. Greeley's hatred of
slavery and his support for high tariffs made him a direct
opponent of southern slaveholding interests. Another reason for

his strong opposition to the extension of slavery was the belief that the new territories were a "safety valve of our industrial and social engine." Greeley, like Carlyle, called for free land for settlers, limited land sales, and unalienable homesteads.[19]

When the passions over slavery nearly erupted into civil war in 1849 and 1850, the Great Compromiser, Henry Clay, with the help of Daniel Webster and Stephen Douglas, managed to delay the "irrepressible conflict" for another decade with the Compromise of 1850. The compromise included a provision that organized Utah as a territory whose citizens, by popular sovereignty, could decide for or against slavery—a principle that would quickly undermine the compromise.

In 1854, Illinois senator Stephen Douglas, seeking to aid the development of the West and to encourage a transcontinental railroad across the central plains, introduced a bill to organize the Nebraska Territory. In an attempt to win southern support, Douglas made two major concessions. First, he agreed that the popular sovereignty clause in the 1850 compromise voided the Missouri Compromise of 1820, which prohibited slavery in the Louisiana Territory north of latitude thirty-six degrees, thirty minutes. Second, Douglas agreed to support the division of the Nebraska Territory into two potential states: Nebraska and Kansas. This would give the South an opportunity to capture at least one as a slave state. Greeley recognized the importance of the struggle in Kansas and vehemently opposed the Kansas-Nebraska Act "from first to last [with] whatever of strength [he] possessed."[20]

Besides the role of reformer, Greeley most treasured his position as a force in Whig politics. His political alliance with Weed and Seward remained harmonious in the early forties. However, as the *Tribune*'s circulation increased and its influence expanded, Greeley exerted more independence and strayed further and further from Weed's control. The triumvirate coop-

William Seward, New York governor, U.S. Senator, secretary of state and Greeley ally. (Courtesy University of Rochester Library)

erated in the 1848 election, with Greeley helping to elect Seward to the Senate. In return, Weed used his influence to have the state legislature select Greeley to complete a term in the House of Representatives. Although he served for only one short session, the new congressman set out to right all wrongs. He introduced legislation to prohibit flogging and eliminate the grog ration in the navy, presented a bill to change the name of the country to Columbia, and opposed slavery whenever possible.

While in the House, Greeley served on the Committee on Public Lands. His effort to use his position on the committee to enact homestead laws reveals much about his attitude toward the West as the land of opportunity and the safety valve. Shortly after assuming his seat, the new congressman introduced a bill that would authorize each landless citizen with a small tract of public land, without cost. When a western congressman asked Greeley why New York's representative expressed interest in the disposal of public, mostly western, lands, Greeley responded that he was interested because he represented more landless people than anyone else in the House.[21]

During his tenure in Congress, Greeley's greatest "contribution" was an attempt to reform the mileage system. Congressmen collected mileage reimbursement based on their "usual" route between Washington and home. Greeley printed, in the *Tribune,* the mileage submitted and reimbursement paid each member versus the mileage by the most direct route to each member's home. His figures revealed that the Senate paid an excess of $14,881.40 for one session, and the House $47,223.80, including an extra $676.80 to Abraham Lincoln. Congressmen expressed outrage, shouting "demagogue" whenever Greeley rose to speak in the House. At least one of his colleagues proposed expelling, or at least censuring, him.[22] By the end of the session he was easily the most unpopular person in Congress. He wrote his friend Griswold of his experience: "I have divided the House into two parties—one that would like to see me extinguished and the other that wouldn't be satisfied without a hand in doing it."[23] Greeley's actions convinced his political partners, Weed and Seward, that "zeal, unregulated by prudence" seriously restricted the congressman's usefulness. Although Seward liked Greeley personally, he considered him temperamentally unsuited for politics. Years later the editor would reflect that his three months in Congress were "among the most profitably employed" of any period in his life. Perhaps making the acquaintance of Abraham Lincoln, Jefferson Davis, Andrew Johnson, Alexander Stephens, and Simon Cameron, who were also members of the Thirtieth Congress, accounted, in part, for Greeley's comment.[24]

By 1854 the issue of the expansion of slavery into the territories had contributed greatly to the impending demise of the Whig Party. Weed and Seward in New York and Lincoln in Illinois were reluctant to bury the corpse, but Greeley acted as one of the moving spirits at a convention held at Saratoga, New York, on August 16, to consider the formation of an antislavery Republican Party. Throughout the convention he stayed in close contact with Weed and followed his suggestions. Greeley also chaired the platform committee whose final document condemned both the extension of slavery and the Kansas-Nebraska Act.

As a reward for his cooperation at the Saratoga convention, Greeley expected Weed's support for the Republican nomination for governor of New York in 1854. Weed explained, however, that the temperance forces supported Myron H. Clark and the "nativists" strongly opposed Greeley.[25] When Greeley then suggested himself as the candidate for lieutenant governor, Weed replied that the party could not run two prohibitionist candidates on the same ticket. Greeley took the rebuff with apparent good will until the Little Villain, Henry Raymond of the rival *New York Times*, captured the Republican candidacy for lieutenant governor. Greeley felt that Weed had betrayed him. Soon thereafter, on November 24, 1854, the rejected candidate wrote a long letter to Seward dissolving the political partnership of Weed, Seward, and Greeley.[26] Although the editor then followed a more independent path, he continued to cooperate with both Weed and Seward until six years later. Greeley's actions at the Republican National Convention in 1860 caused Raymond to refer to the letter and accuse Greeley of being a disgruntled office seeker who opposed Seward's nomination for president to gain revenge for the 1854 disappointment. Greeley, of course, denied the charge.

During the presidential election year of 1856, Weed believed that his friend William Seward could not win that year, so he supported the Pathfinder, John C. Frémont. After vacillating at first, Greeley also endorsed the westerner. Sam Wilkeson, who later became the *Tribune*'s Washington correspondent, revealed to Seward in 1858 one possible reason for Greeley's change of heart. Apparently Frémont had promised, if elected, to appoint Greeley postmaster general.[27] At the Republican convention that nominated Frémont, Greeley help to write the platform, which opposed the extension of slavery and supported a transcontinental railroad. He also published *A History of the Struggle for Slavery Extension* to educate the voters on slavery and the fight to prevent its extension into the West.[28] Even though Frémont lost the election, Republicans, and especially the three former partners, looked with optimism toward 1860.

Greeley saw an opportunity to exploit a rift in the Democratic Party in 1858. Illinois senator Stephen A. Douglas, a presidential aspirant for 1860, criticized the Buchanan administration's handling of popular sovereignty in the territories. Greeley and other Republican leaders began to support Douglas as a means of weakening the Democratic Party. This tactic worked fine in the East but did not coincide with the plans of Illinois Republicans, who hoped to defeat Douglas's bid for reelection. The *Weekly Tribune,* with an estimated circulation in Illinois of ten thousand, was an important political voice in the state.[29] William Herndon, Lincoln's law partner, wrote Greeley a letter to complain. The Republicans in Illinois felt that Greeley and the national organization were willing to "sell out" local party members to further some larger purpose.[30] Greeley apparently replied to Herndon that the Republicans in Illinois were selfish to resist his plan. Herndon reacted to Greeley's charge, calling Douglas infamous, selfish, and the "greatest liar in the world." Herndon informed the editor, "What you call *selfishness* I call *sagacity* of the people snuffing scoundrelism way in the distance."[31] Lincoln sent Herndon east to smooth over the dispute with Greeley. Although the *Tribune* stopped actively supporting Douglas after the visit, the leading Republican journal offered at best lukewarm encouragement to Lincoln's campaign and did not send a reporter to cover the debates. Years later, Greeley still maintained that his strategy had been correct.[32]

Between the 1858 and 1860 elections, the time seemed right for Greeley to make a long-awaited trip across the prairies and plains to California. Although he took every opportunity along the way to give speeches in praise of the Republican Party, his primary purpose, besides the adventure of seeing this vast territory, was to publicize the need for a transcontinental railroad over the central route. Throughout his trip to the West, which began in April 1859, Greeley displayed his reporting skills in long letters to the *Tribune*. His accounts, printed in the newspaper and later published as *An Overland Journey*, focused not only on the flora and fauna of the West but also on the opportunity the area held for farmers.

During his stay in the Denver area, Greeley visited Gregory's Diggings, where he saw gold for himself. Many immigrants to the area were already returning to the East in disappointment when the *Rocky Mountain News* printed Greeley's report of gold at the diggings. So strong was the public's trust of Greeley's word that thousands in the eastbound crowd turned and headed back to the Colorado gold fields. At least one historian credited Greeley with saving the city of Denver.[33]

After Denver, the traveler continued to Salt Lake City, where he interviewed Brigham Young and surveyed the Mormons' irrigation system before heading to California. An attack of painful boils prevented the planned return across the proposed southern route for the railroad and forced Greeley to complete his journey by sea and across the Isthmus of Panama. By October 1859 he was back at his desk praising the Golden State and the proposed transcontinental railroad.

The *Tribune* and its editor continued to grow in importance. By 1860 the weekly, semiweekly, Pacific Coast, and European editions of the paper had a combined circulation of more than three hundred thousand and an estimated readership of more than a million.[34] Horace Greeley, by then, was the most widely read and influential newspaperman in the United States, and perhaps in the world.[35] Wanting to inform his readers, especially those voting in upcoming elections, on the issues he considered most important, he published a treatise entitled *A Political Textbook for 1860.* In addition to all the previous national platforms and the notable speeches of the candidates, this volume updated the struggle since 1856 against slavery's extension and explained the effort to enact the homestead law.[36]

Although Republicans did not select Greeley as a delegate from New York, he attended the 1860 convention in Chicago as a fill-in delegate from Oregon. He was a member of the platform committee and played a leading part in creating the party's platform, a pro-West document that condemned the extension of slavery into the territories and supported free homesteads for settlers and a transcontinental railroad. Greeley supported Edward Bates of Missouri for the presidency. Although his candidate lost, Greeley was visibly elated when the convention denied the nomination to his former partner, Seward. Raymond, trying to assess the blame for Seward's defeat, later credited Greeley with having ten times as much

Editor and Advocate of the West

impact on the convention as "the Blairs and gubernatorial candidates put together."[37]

Lincoln's election in 1860 prompted a parade of power brokers to Springfield, Illinois. Greeley visited the president-elect to vie for control of political appointments in New York and in the Cabinet. According to Charles Dana, assistant editor of the *Tribune* and later assistant secretary of war in Lincoln's administration, Lincoln named Edward Bates as attorney general to satisfy Greeley.[38] Lincoln, however, also appointed Seward as secretary of state and often consulted Weed on political matters. The Rail Splitter was too astute to become embroiled in the infighting of New York politics. Throughout Lincoln's tenure in office, he remained constantly aware of the power of Greeley's press and worked to keep the errant Republican editor placated.

After Lincoln's death, Greeley at first worked with Andrew Johnson. The new president even offered to appoint the editor "Envoy Extraordinary and Minister Plenipotentiary to Austria."[39] Greeley declined the offer, explaining to a friend that he would not go anywhere until after the next presidential election.[40] The *Tribune* and its editor soon became disillusioned with the Reconstruction policies of President Johnson, a Democrat from Tennessee, and aided the Radical Republicans in their attempt to oust him.

Greeley celebrated the election of the Civil War hero Ulysses S. Grant as president in 1868. The new president invited Greeley to the White House to consult on political appointments in New York.[41] The following year, old friend and vice president Schuyler Colfax brought Greeley the news that Grant had offered to appoint Greeley as Minister to England. The editor again refused appointment to a foreign mission. After thanking Colfax for his good opinion and good offices, Greeley explained that his paper needed him much more than the English mission did.[42]

The reform-minded Greeley gradually became disillusioned with Grant, too. By 1872, appalled by the corruption and ineptitude of Grant's administration, Greeley openly opposed his party's president and accepted the presidential nomination of a splinter group, the Liberal Republicans. The Democrats, with no hope of electing a candidate of their own, also nominated this founding member of the Republican Party as their choice for president. Greeley resigned as editor of the *Tribune* and campaigned vigorously through the summer and into the autumn, but early election returns in October presaged Grant's final landslide in November. Election day only confirmed what Greeley already knew.

Horace Greeley never became president, but few presidents contributed more to the opening and development of the West than he. Throughout his long career as the country's most influential journalist, he maintained a vision of the West as the "Land of Opportunity," where yeoman farmers and their young families could go, settle on their own land, and become independent, self-sufficient producers. To make his dream a reality, Greeley used the orator's platform and the press to advocate an expanded homestead policy, slave-free territories, the transcontinental railroad, and utopian socialism. But he first devoted his energy to convincing young men of the virtues of farming and to doing everything he could to improve that profession.

2

EDUCATING FARMERS
FOR THEIR NOBLE PROFESSION

And we say today, as we have ever said, to the young man or woman light of purse but willing of hand, to the farmer or mechanic of increasing family, slender means and dubious prospects, Your true home is in the West! Seek it, and rear your children there to larger opportunities than await them on the rugged hillsides or in the crowded streets of the East!

Horace Greeley

Good *Farming* ***does*** *Pay ... few pursuits afford as good a prospect, as full an assurance, of reward for intelligent, energetic, persistent effort, as this does...I hope I shall thus convince some farmers that draining, irrigation, deep plowing, heavy fertilizing, etc., are not beyond their power.*

Horace Greeley, What I Know of Farming

For Horace Greeley the hope for America's future lay in the West. He, like Thomas Jefferson, envisioned millions of young farmers plowing the western plains. Unlike Jefferson, Greeley hoped farmers would form utopian socialistic communities and trade with the industrial East. The idealistic editor urged young people in the urban centers to go west to find opportunity for themselves, relieve the overcrowding in the cities, and increase the nation's productivity. If "West" was the answer to where New York's poor should go, then "farm" was the answer to what they should do when they got there.

Greeley considered farming not only a noble profession but also the answer to the plight of New York City's poor. Knowing that most city dwellers lacked the skills to succeed in farming, he used the pages of the *Tribune* to educate them in the latest methods and equipment for preserving and enhancing the productivity of their land. As a leading Whig and, later, a founder of the Republican Party, he worked within his party and through the pages of the *Tribune* to fight for a homestead law that would provide land for the would-be farmers, a transcontinental railroad to bring their produce to a national market, and a high tariff to prevent Europeans from underselling them. Greeley also used editorials, letters, and speeches to help create a separate Department of Agriculture that would import new plants and horticulture for American farmers and a land grant act that would create agricultural colleges to teach farmers science and chemistry. To Greeley, education was the

Educating Farmers

key to changing farming from work fit for oxen to a noble vocation and to converting eastern city dwellers into western farmers.

In the fall of 1841 Greeley merged his *New Yorker* magazine, which he had nurtured through the depression, and the *Log Cabin* with a new weekly edition of the *Tribune*. He aimed his weekly at the rural areas not only of New York and New England but also of the developing regions around the Great Lakes and the Great Plains. As the farmers moved west they took their subscriptions of the *Weekly Tribune* with them. These "frontier" farmers provided Greeley with a large natural constituency.[1] Within a year the *Weekly Tribune* had attracted fifteen thousand subscribers. By 1860 this figure had grown to more than two hundred thousand, with an estimated readership of more than one million, mostly farmers in the western and midwestern states. No other editor in the United States approached his readership or his influence among American farmers.[2] The *Weekly Tribune* was the nearest America had to a national newspaper.[3]

Despite being the greatest American newspaper editor in an era of great editors, Greeley regretted that he had not spent his life as a farmer: "All my riper tastes incline to that blessed calling whereby the human family and its humbler auxiliaries are fed."[4] He later added that had his three sons lived to adulthood, he would have advised them to choose farming as their profession. He was certain that no other business held such promise of success. Farming, according to him, encouraged a reverence for honesty and truth and developed a manly character.[5]

The depression of 1837 convinced Greeley that New York City's starving poor should seek their salvation in the country. As the depression lingered into 1842, he directed the city's workers to "Go into the Country" without hesitation or delay.

Unusually warm weather had ripened the grain and hay crops simultaneously, so farmers needed help with their harvest.[6] The following year, he encouraged young men simply to "Go forth into the fields!" Later he added that the "newly settled, thinly peopled country" offered the determined man many chances for each one offered in a crowded city.[7]

He implored the friends of immigrants arriving in the city to help them along "their way West" as quickly as possible. Greeley advised young men and women of "moderate means and resolute energies" or "slender means and dubious prospects" to move West. Later he pointed out that a "strong-minded, willing, handy man" had a much greater chance for success in the newly settled regions of the country than in the cities.[8] He recommended that young farmers, especially those with families, head west.[9]

Explaining the exponential effect of his plan, he claimed that for every urban worker who moved west another would lift himself up from a lower level to take his place. "Even to those workers who will never migrate," he proclaimed, "Free Land at the West would be a great and lasting benefit." He also reassured eastern property owners that the departure of hundreds of thousands of people for the West would increase the value of the property of those who stayed behind.[10]

Greeley occasionally tempered his enthusiasm by admitting that not everyone should migrate, especially those who already had a good farm. He also agreed that not everyone should be a farmer, but added that whereas other vocations would change or entirely disappear, farming would remain consistent.[11] Throughout the rest of his life, he maintained his enthusiasm for the emigration of urban poor to western farms, despite his occasional qualifications. According to him, in 1869 there were at least one hundred thousand men in New York City

Educating Farmers

who should have already settled on a quarter-section of public land, and built a farm for themselves and their families. If they would have moved from the city, they would have "elevated" labor instead of dragging it down.[12]

Realizing that not everyone had the skills and knowledge to become a successful farmer, Greeley determined that he would instruct them. He first undertook to educate himself on the science of agriculture. He regretted the lack of literature available to farmers in his youth, noting that by the time he left the farm at sixteen he had seen neither a magazine devoted to farming nor a book explaining the natural processes of agriculture.[13] Although he still criticized the scarcity of scholarly agricultural works in his later years, he read and recommended what was available. "Let us make the most of what we have, by diffusing, studying, discussing, criticizing, Liebig's Agricultural Chemistry, Dana's Muck Manual, Waring's Elements, and the books that each treat more especially of some department of the farmer's art," he wrote, "making ourselves familiar, first, with the principles, then the methods, of scientific, efficient, successful husbandry."[14] He suggested that young farmers read the latest literature, and buy the books that taught principles rather than methods. Armed with the most current information and his own knowledge of his land, an individual could choose the best fertilizers and minerals to improve his soil.[15]

In 1847 James J. Mapes, a close friend of Greeley's and a frequent contributor to the *Tribune*, bought a run-down farm and worked to restore it through subsoil drainage, fertilization, and crop rotation.[16] In 1853 Greeley followed Mapes's example and bought a seventy-five-acre farm at Chappaqua, New York, about thirty-five miles from downtown New York City. There he tried many of his ideas before recommending them to his readers. His twenty-five acres of woodland received much of his limited spare time. He cut down the black cherry trees ("as they bred caterpillars to infest my Appletrees") and the dogwoods (although they were beautiful in May, they were "no account for timber") but nurtured the sugar maples and white ash.[17] His success with trees on his own farm led to his overzealous endorsement of tree planting in the West. Even in the face of repeated failures on his small plot in Union Colony, Colorado, he steadfastly clung to the idea that trees were the ideal crop for the western prairies.[18]

Greeley experimented with various fertilizers, including "swamp muck, lime, salt, gypsum, bone-dust, and artificial, as well as mineral, manures," to improve his soil. He also dug, blasted, and picked out rocks, built underground drainage systems, and practiced deep-plowing methods to increase production. The farm featured a three-story barn, with a slate roof, built of four to five thousand tons of stone from a nearby slope. The barn would still be standing long after people had forgotten him, he said.[19] Although he admitted his farm had not been profitable, he still considered farming to be a profession that would pay well, explaining that if he could have devoted his time and attention to the farm it would have been lucrative.[20]

Using what he had learned on his Chappaqua farm and what he had read and heard from the few agricultural scholars he had met, Greeley undertook to teach his readers the science of agriculture. He hoped to help transform agriculture from a process of blindly repeating crude, simple, traditional methods to a recognized profession, "as intellectual and dignified as Physic or Law." He encouraged farmers to treat their labors with the same respect a manufacturer or merchant reserved for his business. The lack of thrift displayed by the

Educating Farmers

cultivation of "half-fenced, unmanured, shallow ploughed, late planted, poorly tilled apologies for farms, with no regular rotation of crops," he announced, "would ruin any business to which ruin is possible."[21]

In 1853, the same year he bought the Chappaqua farm, Greeley hired Solon Robinson as agricultural editor for the *Tribune*, a position Greeley would continue to fill with the best men available. Robinson's weekly columns stressed scientific methods and the latest machinery to make farms more productive. The *Tribune* covered everything from crop rotation to a steam-powered manure distribution system. Farmers learned about turnips as cow feed and a variety of ways to increase corn production. Greeley himself contributed to the long list of articles on the latest in horticulture and veterinary medicine and shared tidbits he gleaned from writers around the world.[22]

Some of the best examples of Greeley's agricultural columns appeared in the *Weekly Tribune* throughout 1870. The following year he gathered this agricultural wisdom into a book entitled *What I Know of Farming*. Again he encouraged the urban poor to emigrate to the West, adding that he believed that such a move would make them "more energetic and aspiring" because they would have to rely on themselves as they never had before.[23] Yet he did not advocate striking out on one's own; he stressed the desirability of "cooperative" settlement or moving as a colony. The method used to settle Union Colony in Colorado Territory came close to his ideal (see chapter 6).

Tribune columns throughout the mid-nineteenth century also carried specific instructions for improving farm production while protecting the environment. Unfortunately, because knowledge was limited at the time, some of these instructions may have contributed to the "dust bowl" devastation in the

1930s. Greeley believed that deep plowing, for example, would extend the growing season, conserve precious moisture during droughts, and prevent erosion by helping the soil to absorb rain that otherwise would rush down the hills carrying topsoil with it. He encouraged farmers to plow fewer acres, but to "pulverize" the soil to a depth of twelve to fifteen inches.[24] To properly prepare the soil for planting, according to the *Tribune*'s editor, the farmer should use "a regular subsoil plow of the most approved pattern, attach to it a strong team, and let it follow the breaking-plow in its furrow, lifting and pulverizing the sub-soil to a depth of not less than six inches."[25] When the breaking plow made its next pass through the field, it would turn the topsoil over onto the pulverized subsoil, thus creating a cultivated depth of twelve to fifteen inches. Next, the farmer, with twice the volume of cultivated soil, should apply double the manure to his field. He also recommended fall plowing to increase absorption of winter rains and improve aeration.[26]

After deep plowing, the farmer needed to add nutrients to his soil. Greeley suggested the farmer discover what his soil lacked originally and what subsequent usage had depleted.[27] His knowledge of soil chemistry and his own land would tell him which additives to use. Greeley, because of his thorough devotion to "home industry," recommended that the farmer begin with products found near his farm, including compost and manure, and buy as little as possible. He listed the uses and advantages of gypsum, lime, phosphates, wood ashes, marl, and guano, but concluded that a good farmer would create ten dollars worth of fertilizer for every dollar's worth of commercial fertilizer that he bought.[28]

Farms also needed sufficient water. He urged farmers to make the most of the resources they had and to consider irri-

Educating Farmers

gation to improve their yield. His farsighted views foretold things to come. He wrote of wells in California that could irrigate hundreds of acres and recommended reservoirs to store the excess until "the thirsty earth demanded" it.[29] He presumed that there were at least a half million homesteads in the United States that could benefit from irrigating their crops with the water they had available to them. Calling on knowledge gained while traveling in the West, Greeley expressed confidence that there were areas along the Carson, the Humbolt, and other western streams where ten to fifty thousand dollars invested in dams, locks, and canals would return 50 percent annually and increase the value of the surrounding property.[30] He acknowledged that farmers who had grown up in the East stuck to the ways of their fathers and rejected irrigation. But, he pointed out, times had changed, the dense forests that surrounded most farms in the past had disappeared and been replaced by hot, parching summer winds. "Even though our grandfathers did not, we *do* need and may profit by Irrigation," he wrote.[31] The experiences of the settlers in Union Colony in the 1870s and farmers in California in the twentieth century proved the wisdom of his words.

Greeley also advocated natural methods to control insects. Estimating that insects destroyed more than $100 million in crops every year, he advised farmers to protect birds, their best allies in the "inglorious warfare" against insects. They should teach their children and hired hands to respect birds ("except hawks"), form neighborhood associations to defend insect-eating birds, and pass laws to punish cowards with guns, who killed "every unsuspecting robin or thrush" they could find. Although he was sure the wanton killing of birds was a primary cause of increased insect damage, he blamed at least half the loss on farmers' failure to plow deeply, use sufficient fertilizers, and conscientiously rotate their crops. Both protecting insect-eating birds and employing more scientific methods of cultivation would, he believed, greatly reduce insect damage.[32]

In his 1870 columns, Greeley renewed his campaign to motivate farmers to plant trees. He wrote earlier of his own experiences on his farm at Chappaqua, New York. By fencing out the cattle to protect the young, tender saplings and by judiciously pruning and cutting the adult trees, he felt that he had greatly improved his woods.[33] If a farmer had a tract of woodland or a piece of land too poor for crops, Greeley urged him to protect it from cattle and plant choice trees. The owner should tend his woods by cutting down trees that had stopped growing or had begun to decay, thus allowing the land to produce more and better trees. Greeley asserted that a farmer near a city could make more money growing timber instead of grain, with less effort.[34] He also claimed that people on the plains and in the Great Basin would profit more from planting groves of choice timber than by working the richest veins of ore in the nearby mountains.[35]

Greeley's enthusiasm led to exaggerated expectations of reclaiming all the great deserts of the temperate and torrid zones through irrigation and tree planting.[36] His passion caused him to accept, then espouse, the fallacy that tree planting would increase rainfall. Although no one could fully explain "the interdependence of these two blessings," he considered it to be a fact and supported it by repeating a story he had heard about the Mormons. After they had planted trees over considerable sections of Utah, summer rains increased, the level of the Salt Lake rose, and "the equilibrium of rainfall with evaporation in the Great Basin [was] fully restored," or, rather, rainfall was now "taking the lead."[37] The idea that

Educating Farmers

"rain-fall followed the plow" became widely accepted in the 1870s and 1880s, a period of increased rainfall in the plains, and prompted farmers to move deeper and deeper into arid regions. Consequently, the return of normal rainfall levels ruined thousands of farmers. Horace Greeley inadvertently contributed to this disaster.

Although he was grossly mistaken in asserting that planting trees was a cure for dry conditions on the plains, he accurately depicted the ecological value of trees. He described the disastrous effects of "scathing winds" on delicate fruits trees and other crops after the destruction of the "genial, hospitable" forests. He added that stripping the hills of trees not only made timber more expensive but also caused streams to "become desolating torrents" in the rainy season and to dry up in the summer and fall. If land owners would plant trees along the tops of ridges and sides of ravines on their property, he suggested, more grass would grow on their land and they could avoid erosion. He lamented that farmers had stripped the hills of trees and called on his countrymen to "unitedly cease to do evil and learn to do well in relation to trees."[38]

Greeley also undertook to inform farmers of the latest inventions designed to increase productivity. He felt sure that the equipment already available to make work easier and more productive would surprise most farmers. The number and variety of innovative machines for plowing, fertilizing, planting, weeding, and harvesting would probably surpass most people's imagination, he believed. Although he recognized the value of this new machinery, he realized that the ordinary individual could not afford to purchase everything he needed. The answer to this and many similar problems was "Cooperation" or "Association." He suggested that neighbors meet and decide to each buy a different piece of equipment, with the agreement that each would then be able to use any of the equipment bought by the others. With this arrangement, a farmer would benefit nearly as much as if he owned all the equipment, but at a mere fraction of the cost.[39]

He also envisioned harnessing steam to power farm machinery. He predicted great inventions in the next forty years, including a steam-powered engine, operated by one man, that would pull six to twelve plows and plow twelve to twenty-five acres in one day.[40] Although the gasoline-powered farm tractor still lay years in the future, Greeley wrote of the need for a "locomotive" that could easily travel over plowed fields and respond to its "manager's touch" as readily as a team of horses. This new machine could be a portable power source that readily operated a plow, a harrow, a wagon, a mill, a mower, or a stump-puller. He believed that his children would live to see such an invention.[41] His foresight surely smoothed the way for farmers' acceptance of the modern farm machinery that appeared in the last quarter of the nineteenth century.

In addition to instructing readers through the pages of his newspaper, Greeley took his educational campaign to a national level. He enjoyed influence within his party that extended beyond his role as the editor of his party's leading newspaper. He exercised his power in both roles to fight for farmer's causes, especially for an independent Department of Agriculture and for land-grant agricultural colleges. A national Department of Agriculture, with an annual budget of one hundred thousand dollars could, Greeley argued, import enough seeds and plants from the Far East to provide this country with millions of dollars in new products. He also claimed that for the cost of two voyages to China, Americans could have a tea plant that would produce a domestically grown tea that would be better and cheaper than tea imported from the Orient.[42] A Department of Agriculture could also promote science in agriculture, including the use of irrigation, manuring, deep plowing, and draining. This would increase national production by 50 percent.[43] Even after the creation of the department in 1862, Greeley continued to push to give it stronger powers, competent direction, and a national outlook.

His newspaper and the Department of Agriculture could only produce limited results, Greeley believed. The American farmer, whose life's work required a thorough knowledge of the sciences, needed a comprehensive curriculum from elementary school through college dedicated to the science of agriculture. Geology and chemistry, he believed, were "the natural bases of a sound, practical knowledge of things." A farmer needed a thorough understanding of his soil—the chemicals, minerals, and elements of which it was composed—but the schools of Greeley's day did not provide this knowledge.[44] In 1851 he decried the lack of colleges for farmers, although farming was, he said, the most indispensable of all professions[45] and agriculture was a science that deserved the same status as other professions.

In keeping with his natural fiscal conservatism, Greeley at first envisioned a privately financed industrial college that taught not only chemistry, mineralogy, and agriculture but also mechanical science and "useful arts." The institution could both educate and produce marketable wares that would help to sustain the college. Although he did not advocate governmental support for his program in 1844, by the 1850s he realized the national government would have to help.[46] The suggestion of federal support for agricultural colleges met a wall of opposition from southern states'-rights congressmen throughout the 1850s. Finally, in 1859, both houses of Congress passed Vermont congressman Justin S. Morrill's bill granting public lands to all states to help create and maintain colleges to teach agriculture and the mechanical arts. According to Greeley, the measure passed even though "every Filibuster, Cuba-stealer and active Slavery Propagandist said Nay." When President James Buchanan vetoed Morrill's bill, Greeley assured his readers that despite the president's publicly expressed doubts about the bill's constitutionality, Buchanan acted as a puppet of the slave owners, who opposed education for the workers.[47]

Greeley continued his call for a land-grant college bill, claiming its benefit could not be overstated.[48] The measure remained dead until Buchanan left office and Southern opposition withdrew from Congress. Then, in 1862, the Morrill Land Grant College Bill[49] passed the Senate by a thirty-two to seven margin and the House by a vote of ninety to twenty-five. Greeley was ecstatic. He called the measure an "augury of wide and lasting good" and claimed that if only five colleges resulted from the act, it would be worth the years of struggle and the cost of administration.[50] President Abraham Lincoln signed the measure into law on July 2, 1862.

The act granted each state thirty thousand acres of public land for each of its senators and representatives in Congress. Income from the sale of this land would support agricultural and mechanical arts colleges. Historian Allan Nevins called the enactment of the land-grant measure "an immortal moment in the history of higher education in America and the world" and acknowledged Greeley's contribution to the event.[51] Many of the sixty-nine land-grant colleges created under Morrill's act grew into major universities.

Because much of the public lands destined for sale to support the colleges lay in the West, Greeley expected some opposition there. He reminded westerners that the East had

Educating Farmers

generously supported a homestead law and the transcontinental railroad bill, so he trusted that the West would not begrudge this small contribution to the agricultural colleges. The passage of the Morrill Land Grant College Act opened "a new and brighter era" for the West, and Greeley promised, "We will try to send her more farmers and better because of that beneficent measure."[52] Meanwhile, Greeley also worked to provide these new farmers with free land.

3

ADVOCATING LAND REFORM
AND THE HOMESTEAD ACT

RESOLVED: *That we protest against any sale or alienation to others of the public lands held by actual settlers, and against any view of the free-homestead policy which regards the settlers as paupers or suppliants for public bounty; and we demand the passage by Congress of the complete and satisfactory homestead measure which has already passed the House.*

Republican Party platform, 1860

Every thousand hardy, efficient workers who floated West to locate on Free Lands would leave places open for as many others; and these, taking a step upward, would leave room for the advancement of as many more, and so on. Even to those workers who will never migrate, Free Land at the West would be a great and lasting benefit.

Horace Greeley

The Homestead Act signed into law by Abraham Lincoln in 1862, was not only the fulfillment of the promise made at the 1860 Republican National Convention but also the culmination of a struggle that had begun twenty-five years earlier. One of the people at the forefront of that effort was Horace Greeley. His pursuit of relief for New York City's poor naturally led him to the issue of land reform. Between the Panic of 1837 and the passage of the Homestead Law of 1862, Greeley evolved from a strong conservative who supported land speculation to a utopian socialist who advocated free land for the masses, including noncitizen immigrants. Initially, he implored idle workers to leave the city to labor on others' farms. Gradually he came to believe that only the deed to their own land would allow the poor to become self-sufficient, productive citizens. It was not simply that Greeley's ideas about property rights changed, but that the possibilities of reform slowly changed him.

A political and fiscal conservative, the young Greeley believed that capital and labor formed a harmonious relationship and an industrious, hardworking, honest worker could rise to the top. The federal government, according to Greeley, should limit itself to keeping order, correcting abuse, and preventing injustice between citizens. Its only active role should be helping the business class develop the nation's economic potential. Greeley supported Henry Clay's American system based on high tariffs and internal improvements. He even con-

Advocating Land Reform

doned the practice of buying land, holding it until the price increased, then reselling it to would-be settlers.[1] His values coincided with the conservative Whig platform of the time, so he was a natural to edit the party's *Jeffersonian* in 1837–38 and the *Log Cabin* during the 1840 campaign.[2]

The panic that began near the end of 1836 directly affected Horace Greeley. Subscriptions for his *New Yorker* dropped immediately and those who continued to subscribe seldom paid. His immediate loss was one hundred dollars a week, which quickly became an enormous burden. By writing columns and editorials for other journals, he barely managed to sustain himself, his bride, and his magazine. Near the end of 1837, when Whig Party boss Thurlow Weed offered him one thousand dollars to publish the *Jeffersonian*, Greeley jumped at the opportunity. But his own economic predicament improved hardly at all until after the birth of the *Tribune* in April 1841 and the eventual passing of the national crisis.

Despite his own woes, the despair of the tens of thousands of homeless and hungry in New York's streets and alleys touched Greeley deeply. The *New Yorker*'s few remaining subscribers must have noticed the change in the editor's attitude. Throughout 1837 and 1838 he filled the pages of the magazine and the *Jeffersonian* with pleas for poor workers to move to the country or the West.[3] He later recalled the agony of seeing able-bodied men and women asking not for charity but for the opportunity to work.[4] Noting that twenty thousand mechanics and thirty thousand seamstresses in New York City were without work, he encouraged laborers "to take up the march for the new country."[5] Even for those who lacked investment capital, the West offered an advantage. Greeley asserted that even a little capital would go further in the West than in the crowded eastern cities.[6]

In 1842 Greeley believed that the city's economy could not recover for at least another year. Having grown up on a farm, he urged the laborers of New York not to wait for the additional distress the winter would bring but to "Fly—scatter through the country—go to the Great West—anything rather than remain here."[7] Willing workers would fair much better in a "young and thriving" community than in the eastern cities.[8]

He also believed that the constant influx of immigrants fleeing starvation in Europe further aggravated problems, so he demanded a restriction of immigration and a revision of the naturalization laws, suggestions he would later criticize when brought forth by the American Party, or "nativists."[9] As an advocate for the poor and a spokesman for the Whigs, Greeley soon became embroiled in the land-reform controversy. After the birth of the *Tribune* in 1841 and the merging of the *New Yorker* and the *Log Cabin* into the *Weekly Tribune* a few months later, both Greeley's audience and influence grew until he soon became the mid-nineteenth century's most important spokesperson for free farms for settlers.

The federal government's method of raising revenue by selling public land in large blocks to people who had the money to pay had already provoked criticism before Greeley became involved. Three different but interrelated land-reform programs dominated public discussion for two decades after 1825: distribution, graduation, and preemption. Supporters of distribution, including Henry Clay and Horace Greeley, were content to see the current method continued, except the federal government should restrict the sale of public lands in the territories and newer states to actual settlers and distribute the profits from those sales to the older states based on their representation in Congress.

The other two plans were more radical and had greater support in the West. Graduation would reduce the price of

Advocating Land Reform

government land that had been on the market for an extended period of time. Backers argued that the unsold parcels would be marginal land, which should be available to poor settlers at lower prices. Many westerners also supported preemption, which would allow farmers who had settled on public land before it became available for purchase to have a preemptive right to buy that land when the federal government designated it for sale. Supporters for each plan gained new fuel for their fires in 1837.

The impact of the depression on the nation's poor, especially in the industrial cities of the Northeast, prompted even more drastic suggestions for the disposal of public lands. Shortly after 1840 a faint cry arose from a small group of radicals proclaiming every citizen's right to enough land to feed himself and his family. These supporters of a homestead law soon swept the other land-reform measures aside and pushed their cause to the forefront. Because of stiff opposition from southerners, who viewed small plots of free land as a means for undermining slavery, the measure had to wait until 1862, after its detractors had withdrawn from Congress, before it became law. Horace Greeley, who came to believe that a small farm in the West was the answer to the prayers of New York City's poor, became the voice for the homestead bill and a key figure in its eventual success. But the idea of free land evolved slowly.

Although Thomas Hart Benton, Democratic senator from Missouri and advocate of western development, introduced a graduation bill in December 1825 as a means of making marginal lands available to settlers who had little hard cash, the land-reform controversy focused on preemption versus distribution until 1844. The fiscally conservative Greeley expressed his and many other Whigs' disgust with preemption in the columns of the *Tribune* in 1843. He defined preemption as trespass, called it a "curse on the West and the whole country," and claimed that it would destroy the industry, morals and prosperity of the West.[10]

Opponents of distribution, on the other hand, argued that because the proceeds from the sale of public lands and import taxes were the two primary sources of government income, any decrease in proceeds from land sales would trigger an increase in import taxes. Greeley advocated high import taxes to protect fledgling American industries, so protection for northern manufacturing interests was directly tied to distribution of the profits from the sale of western lands. Southern Democrats perceived distribution as a front for protectionism and, therefore, as a threat to the South's vigorous trade with Great Britain and Europe. Whigs from the South joined the Democrats in fighting any proposal that would increase import taxes.

With such clearly drawn battle lines, it is surprising that the two sides reached a compromise that incorporated both preemption and distribution. When Congress reconvened in May 1841, Greeley hoped that Henry Clay, "Heaven bless him," had returned to Washington ready to champion a distribution bill.[11] Clay, always the Great Compromiser, helped to blend the two causes into the Preemption Act of 1841, which became law with bipartisan support. The principal provision of the measure permitted a single male adult or any head of household to preempt 160 acres of public land and then pay the minimum price of $1.25 an acre when the federal government opened the land for settlement. Ten percent of the proceeds from the sale of the land would go to the state in which the land was located, the federal government distributing the other 90 percent among all states in proportion to their representation in Congress. To satisfy southern concerns about the tariff, the bill stated that if the tax rate exceeded 20 per-

Advocating Land Reform

cent, the distribution portion of the measure would automatically be suspended. Greeley accepted the preemption feature, even though he had abhorred the idea three years earlier, and praised "the Distribution Bill" (as he preferred to call it) as the most important measure Congress had considered in 1841.[12]

The spirit of compromise and the *Tribune*'s support for the law were short-lived, however. Greeley's personal social awakening had coincided with a shift in Whig Party politics. Blaming Democratic economic policies for many of the problems of the time, Whigs moved from their traditional conservative, upper-class leanings to soliciting support from the working classes during the 1840 campaign. The pages of the *Log Cabin* suggested that a stronger currency and a protective tariff would raise the standard of living for the American worker.[13] This strategy succeeded; but when newly elected Whig president William Henry Harrison died soon after taking office, John Tyler, a southerner who opposed distribution, ascended to the presidency. Party leader Henry Clay, whom Greeley admired, trusted, and "profoundly loved," confronted Tyler in a battle for a higher tariff in 1842.[14] The president agreed to sign the bill but demanded that the Whigs abandon the distribution of the proceeds from the sale of public lands. Greeley, realizing that his idol lacked the strength to force the president's hand, accepted that distribution was a dead issue. Although he continued to be an ardent Clay supporter, Greeley began to differ with the Whig leader on land policy and resumed his condemnation of preemption, denouncing the practice as "squatting" and "trespass."[15]

Congressional supporters of graduation, meanwhile, renewed Benton's 1825 suggestion for reducing the price on less-desirable public lands during the 1844 session. But opponents, including Greeley, saw graduation as a scheme to line the pockets of speculators at the expense of eastern taxpayers. The *Tribune*'s editor warned readers that they must stay alert and "foil the demagogues" who were relentlessly trying to "squander the public lands." He asserted that a bill that reduced the price of public lands to twenty-five cents an acre or made the lands free would allow wealthy capitalists or speculators to monopolize entire counties. Ultimately, the buyers would rent the land to tenant farmers or hold it for resale at exorbitant profit. Greeley considered public lands as not only a source of federal income but also as "the great regulator of the relations of Labor and Capital, the safety valve of our industrial and social engine." He depicted the poor as victims of those who claimed to act in their behalf.[16]

When the bill came up for debate again in 1846, Greeley described it as "full of mischief and injustice" and called it "a bill to discourage and prevent all payment for the public lands, and enable speculators to get them ultimately for a song."[17] Despite his best efforts, graduation became law in 1854. Although Congress restricted the measure to those who would actually settle on the land and till the soil, enforcement proved to be impossible. Greeley's dire predictions came true. Before the Homestead Act of June 2, 1862 repealed the graduation act, speculators acquired millions of acres of desirable land at prices far below $1.25 an acre.[18]

Convinced that the gravity of New York's laborers' poverty required new answers, Greeley began to listen to radical suggestions. George Henry Evans, a labor leader, proposed easing the workers' burden by offering them free land in the West.[19] Thomas Carlyle's *Past and Present,* which Greeley called the "greatest book the century has so far produced," visualized land as the source of the nation's wealth and encouraged migration from the cities to the country.[20] These and

Advocating Land Reform

similar ideas formed the core of the National Reform movement during the mid-1840s. Although Greeley relished his position in the Whig Party too much to give his unqualified support to the movement, he presented its arguments in the pages of the *Tribune.* In 1845, for example, he applauded the reformers' call for the government to cease selling public land and instead survey the land, divide it into 160-acre quarter-sections, and make it available free of charge to actual settlers.[21] A section of 640 acres was the usual method of measuring large areas. Later, when a rival newspaper pointed out that such a proposal would conflict with the slave system, Greeley frankly admitted that he supported land reform that promoted settlement by free labor, not slaveholders.[22]

Much to the chagrin of his political partners Thurlow Weed and William Seward, by the latter half of the 1840s Horace Greeley's ideas on land reform became more and more radical. In 1847, undoubtedly remembering the loss of the family farm of his youth, Greeley "rejoiced" at a proposal in the New York legislature to exempt family homesteads from foreclosure for debt. Although he doubted the bill would pass immediately, he predicted that it would ultimately succeed.[23] The following year he exhorted Congress to set aside, without cost, at least forty acres of public land as a home for every landless man in America. Furthermore, he urged the federal government to limit sales to 160-acre parcels and prohibit any but actual settlers from purchasing public land.[24] Earlier he had criticized Andrew Johnson's 1845 proposed homestead bill because it lacked safeguards against speculation. He charged that presenting a clear title to a quarter-section of public land to any claimant would allow speculators to accumulate even larger tracts of land at a lower cost.[25] From this time on, Greeley criticized any land-reform measure that did not contain safeguards against the "evils of speculation." His political thinking had changed dramatically in the decade following the Panic of 1837.

In 1848 New York Whigs, led by Thurlow Weed, selected Greeley to complete a short term in the House of Representatives. He carried his fight for land reform to the floor of the House. Shortly after taking his seat he introduced a bill authorizing a small plot of public land to each landless citizen without charge.[26] Although he believed the bill to be "right," he acknowledged that there was no chance Congress would approve it.[27] While in Washington he served on the Committee on Public Lands, which he defined as a group of honest men determined to protect the public from speculators' greed.[28] Although he later described his few months in Congress as being the most fulfilling period of his life, in truth the House hardly considered his land-reform bill and he accomplished little.

Greeley continued his campaign after he left Washington and formally resumed his position as the *Tribune*'s editor (a position he never really left). He called for Congress to act to prevent future sales of public lands to all but actual settlers and to impose conditions that would prevent one person from accumulating large plots. No one should be able to acquire more than 160 acres, except at an enhanced price, he argued. The federal government must also make at least forty acres of land available to the landless free of charge. In other words, he explained, Washington should transfer the title to public lands only to those who needed the land and would live there.[29]

Greeley achieved one of his goals when the New York legislature passed the Homestead Exemption Law on April 11, 1850. He claimed the new law would not only make thousands of young people frugal and additional thousands of older

Advocating Land Reform

people independent but also practically guarantee every family's right to a home.[30]

For the next twelve years he focused his land-reform energy on a homestead bill that would provide free land for the poor and thwart speculation. As a political leader and editor of his party's most powerful newspaper, Greeley stayed in close contact with several congressmen and showered them with advice on the issue. Members of Congress, often under his direct prodding, offered a new bill at almost every session, but to no avail.[31]

He also continued to use his mightiest weapon, his editorials in the New York *Tribune,* to garner public support and apply pressure on the nation's political leaders. "Land for the landless," Greeley proclaimed, was a "corner stone of Republican institutions." In 1850, two years after the war with Mexico had ended, Congress considered a bounty land bill that would provide free land to veterans of the war. Greeley criticized the bill for not opening its provisions to all citizens.[32] He assured his readers that the measure would benefit "speculators and land sharks" not the veterans: "The tree is shaken in their name, but it is in Wall St. and similar patriotic localities that the fruit will be gathered and devoured." He also argued that the bill would interfere with the building of a Pacific railroad. The only ray of hope he saw in the bill was that the land grab might be large enough to create a backlash and destroy the speculators. After the Military Bounty Land Bill had passed both houses of Congress, Greeley estimated that it would transfer at least twenty million acres to speculators. The articulate editor lamented, "O long-suffering People! long-plundering Congress! when shall we have that most righteous, most necessary act making the Public Lands Free in quarter-sections to Actual Settlers alone?"[33]

The speculator was the nemesis of land reform in Greeley's eyes. He praised a law in Wisconsin that limited a person to 640 acres of land within the state.[36] He also supported Senator William Seward's proposal to restrict the area of public lands that one individual could buy and reserve the lands for settlers. If people did not have the means to purchase land, they should be able to obtain a small parcel to improve and cultivate without cost. Seward also wanted the land secure from foreclosure.[35] These features encapsulated Greeley's ideas on land reform.

Besides Seward, Democrats Andrew Johnson of Tennessee, Stephen Douglas of Illinois, and Sam Houston of Texas alternately introduced bills to provide free land for settlers. Each met defeat. Senator Isaac P. Walker of Wisconsin tried a different tack in 1852 with a measure that would cede public lands to the states in which they were located, on the condition that those states convey the land in limited quantities to actual occupants for a minimal cost.[36] Like its predecessors, Walker's proposal failed. The *Tribune* called the Senate's rejection a "slap in the face" to land reform and derided the upper house for then abetting speculators in bounty warrants.[37]

In 1854 Congress debated between a homestead bill and the graduation bill discussed above. Greeley described the homestead bill as measure to provide small tracts of public land to actual farmers, whereas the graduation bill would transfer large tracts of the same land to speculators. Even though he considered the homestead measure worthy of passage in a fair vote, he acknowledged the strength of its opponents: "The speculators in Lands and in Land Warrants, or Military Claims" and "the Railroad jobbers whose name is legion, and whose swallow is capacious enough for empires." Greeley warned that passage of the graduation bill would mean

Advocating Land Reform

inexpensive land initially but exorbitant prices later. He feared the Senate would "stifle" the homestead bill and pass the graduation bill.[38] His prediction proved correct.

The voting pattern on the 1854 homestead bill showed an interesting change. Because the Kansas–Nebraska Act of that same year had reawakened the sectional conflict over the spread of slavery into the territories, support for the homestead bill began to divide along northern and southern lines. Congressmen from the slave states feared that small tracts of free land would attract antislavery voters to the West and upset the slave state–free state balance in Congress.[39] The bitter struggle in and over Kansas overshadowed the homestead question for the next five years.

After the failure of the 1854 effort, the homestead bill lay dormant until 1859, when Pennsylvania's Galusha Grow reintroduced the measure in the House of Representatives. The combined votes of the members from the Northeast and the West passed it over the opposition of the South by a vote of 120 to 76. This news elated Greeley, who asserted that the enactment of such a law fifteen years earlier would have prevented much public corruption and increased the power and happiness of the entire country.[40] The bill moved on to the Senate, where it languished in committee. Greeley continued the fight: "We believe the passage of this bill would add tens of thousands immediately, and hundreds of thousands ultimately, to the number of our producers of wealth, subtracting from the number of our paupers and the famishing crowd vainly struggling in the great cities."[41]

Greeley even argued that if one hundred thousand people moved from the eastern cities to the West, property values for all the arable land in between would improve. The resultant increased trade between the two regions would also en-

*Galusha Grow, Pennsylvania congressman, father of the Homestead Law.
(Courtesy the National Archives)*

Advocating Land Reform

hance the property values in New York City and the surrounding area. He ridiculed those who predicted that if the bill passed business owners would be unable to find workers and abandoned farms would blight the countryside. Instead, he reassured his readers, "We shall not be able . . . to even drain our great cities of their surplus scores of thousands; but some will go, and leave more room and better chances for those who remain."[42] He later claimed that the passage of the homestead bill would move hundreds of thousands of people from the roles of pauper to positions as producers of wealth.[43] His eloquent words fell on deaf ears as Vice President John Breckenridge, a southern Democrat, cast the tie-breaking vote that prevented the measure from coming to a vote before the Senate adjourned.

Greeley was adamant that the measure should not die. He described the distress in the poverty-ridden urban centers, where most people accumulated children "faster than property." If the public lands were free, he argued, tens of thousands of these poor people would find some means to reach the free land and survive until they could make the land pay. He proclaimed that if a homestead law enticed one million poor people to move from the older states to the West, both areas would benefit equally. "The crush of competition in these swarming hives of population would be somewhat lessened in intensity; and those we missed as competitors would reappear to us in the more benignant attitude of customers."[44]

On 15 February 1860, Grow reintroduced his homestead bill. Six days of heated debate followed after the measure reached the floor of the House, with supporters and opponents divided along anti- and proslavery lines. It passed by a vote of 115 to 65, with one negative vote from a free state and one in support from the South. In the Senate, Andrew Johnson pushed through a bill designed to overcome constitutional objections to free land by charging twenty-five cents an acre. Several southerners backed the measure, and it passed the Senate by a margin of 44 to 8. After a long conference, the two houses compromised on a bill that would sell the public lands at twenty-five cents an acre, in parcels not to exceed 160 acres, to heads of family who lived on the land for at least five years. The measure also included provisions for preemption and graduation, but only for those who resided on the land. The House approved the bill 115 to 51 and the Senate 36 to 2.[45]

Even though Greeley considered this to be "a half loaf" because it did not provide free land and included preemption and graduation clauses, he was pleased because he saw the bill as a blow to speculators who held large tracts of land and others who had gambled in land warrants.[46] Greeley's joy quickly turned to outrage when President James Buchanan vetoed the bill on "constitutional" grounds. "Mr. Buchanan must be a near relative of him whom the Yankee characterized as having 'remarkable winning ways to make people hate him,'" Greeley said. "The North-West was already so unanimously averse to him that he could only intensify its dislike into hatred; but that seems an object worthy of his ambition." He characterized Buchanan as having no sympathy for the poor and as interested only in benefiting the speculators. Greeley assured his readers that Abraham Lincoln, whom the Republicans had recently nominated as their presidential candidate for the forthcoming election, would never veto such a bill.[47]

The Republican Party, in the meantime, had held its presidential convention in Chicago. Horace Greeley served on the platform committee, and his imprint on paragraph 13, the plank that derided speculators and called for the passage of a

Advocating Land Reform

homestead law, is obvious. In a letter to his friend Schuyler Colfax, Greeley later referred to this "plank in the Chicago Platform which I fixed exactly to my own liking."[48] The Republican Party was on the record in support of the homestead. Illinois representative Owen Lovejoy, another strong backer of a homestead act, later proclaimed that this plank in the Republican platform made possible Lincoln's election in November 1860.[51]

Despite Lovejoy's claim and Greeley's assessment that a homestead act was the greatest issue in the West, "stronger than any party," the threat of secession and war dominated the presidential campaign during the fall of 1860. The homestead act was an important but minor issue. Greeley, seeking support for his party's nominee, used the pages of the *Tribune* to explain the importance of land reform to both the East and the West, repeating the familiar argument that western farmers would trade their produce for eastern manufactured goods.[50] Lincoln's election, however, did not mean the immediate enactment of the measure.

When the "lame duck" Congress met in December 1860, the House of Representatives quickly passed a homestead bill and moved it on to the Senate. Greeley doubted the Senate would act as quickly, but he assured his readers that the upper house would also approve the bill. If, then, the president would sign it, the woes of Kansas would be over, prosperity would return to the great Northwest, and "we may congratulate the industrious poor of the cities and of all the Atlantic hives of population on the opening of a way of escape from their ever-recurring embarrassments and sufferings, through the dearth of employment and the frequency of Panics." The resulting increase of "cultivators" would also provide larger markets for the manufacturing areas of the Northeast and add to the prosperity of the entire country.[51] Despite the editor's assurances, the bill died in a Senate committee.

When Congress returned to Washington for the special session during the summer of 1861, Representative Cyrus Aldrich of Minnesota introduced a homestead measure very similar to Grow's 1859 bill. The Speaker of the House referred the bill to the Agriculture Committee for study. With the southern opposition having already withdrawn from Congress and President Lincoln an advocate of free land for settlers in the White House, backers were confident that some form of homestead law would be enacted. Pressing Civil War business delayed action on the bill in 1861, but the committee quickly reported the measure back to the House when Congress met in regular session at the beginning of the new year. Just before the House took up the matter, the *Tribune* prompted Congress to act quickly, noting that proponents and opponents had debated every question involved until any citizen with normal intelligence knew the details well enough to vote on the bill without further discussion. The editorial then returned to a familiar argument: "Every smoke rising from a new opening in the wilderness marks the foundation of a new feeder to Commerce and the Revenue."[52] The full House gave its approval on 28 February 1862 by a vote of 107 to 16.

As the bill moved to the upper house, Greeley focused on that body. He reminded Senate Republicans of the homestead plank in the 1860 party platform, which he described as an "old-fashioned document" filled with valuable truth. He then repeated his claim that the cities were full of men who would gladly work, if only work were available. A homestead law would correct this inequity and provide many of these idle hands an opportunity to work.[53] On 6 May 1862 the Senate, by a vote of thirty-three to seven, passed an amended version of

Advocating Land Reform

the bill, adding military bounties for veterans. The negative votes in both houses came from border states. After a limited debate between the two branches of Congress, both accepted a compromise that included most of the Senate's changes. Greeley congratulated the Congress and the country on the success of one of the most beneficial and important reforms ever attempted, "a reform calculated to diminish sensible the number of paupers and idlers and increase the proportion of working, independent, self-subsisting farmers in this land evermore."[54]

After the president signed the homestead bill into law on 20 May 1862, the *Tribune*'s editor explained the virtues of the new measure in response to a letter to the paper. He ended his article with the familiar cry for young men, poor men, and widows to determine to have a home of their own. He recommended that they purchase one in the East, if they could pay for it. If they lacked the means to buy a farm, then Greeley invited them to "make one in the broad and fertile West!"[55]

The Homestead Act of 1862 allowed any head of a household, twenty-one years old or a veteran of at least fourteen days in the United States military, who was a citizen or had filed forms announcing his intention to become a citizen, and who had not borne arms against the United States to claim 160 acres of public land for their own use. They must live on the land for five years before they could acquire title. The land was exempt from sale for any debt contracted before the homesteaders staked their claim. If the claimant left the homestead for more than six months, the land reverted back to the government. The filing fee was ten dollars, and the law continued the preemption clause that had been in effect since 1841.[56]

Five years after the Homestead Act became law, Greeley asserted that at no time in history had it ever been so easy for poor people to obtain their own land. A hardworking man, with little or no money, could move West and acquire clear title to an eighty-acre farm within ten years.[57] The new law had even opened this western "land of opportunity" to the newly freed blacks. Speaking to a racially mixed audience at the African Church in Richmond, Virginia, Greeley encouraged whites and blacks to forget their animosities and differences and to work together to unify the nation. He urged the young, newly emancipated blacks to "reconstruct" themselves by moving West, homesteading land, and becoming independent, self-sufficient farmers.[58]

Greeley's enthusiasm for the new law proved to be premature and overly optimistic. His was an idealistic and utopian vision that never came to pass. Modern historians have disagreed on the value of the Homestead Act. Although acknowledging that it had weaknesses, Everett Dick proclaimed, "The Homestead Act had the greatest social impact of all the land laws; for nearly three quarters of a century it offered land for the landless. At home and far overseas the thrilling announcement of free land was heard."[59] While Fred A. Shannon, another historian of that era, asserted, "In its operation, the Homestead Act could hardly have defeated the hopes of the enthusiasts of 1840–1860 more completely if the makers had actually drafted it with that purpose in mind."[60]

Despite Greeley's dream that free land would solve the problems of the urban poor, emigrants needed more than land to build a farm. Settlers who moved west needed money to travel to the public lands, more money for the registration fees, still more money for seed, equipment, and livestock, and yet more money to sustain themselves and their families until they could cultivate, harvest, and sell the first crop. Homesteading was not for the poor or the meek. Also, the new law, despite all the precautions, did not protect the land from speculators. Loopholes allowed speculators to acquire large tracts by using agents who homesteaded the land for six months, then paid $1.25 an acre to obtain the deed to the property. The deed then quickly passed to the speculator.

One of the greatest failings of the Homestead Act of 1862 was that it did not work in the semiarid area west of the hundredth meridian, the region containing most of the public land. Farmers tried to apply a law drawn with visions of Illinois and Iowa in mind to Kansas, Nebraska, and the Dakotas. On the plains, a farmer could not live on 160 acres. Later amendments attempted to remedy the oversight, but farmers would have to learn a new agriculture before they could grow crops in the West.

Despite these shortcomings, the Homestead Act contributed greatly to the settling of the West. By the end of the nineteenth century, homesteaders had claimed more than seventy million acres in the Great Plains.[61] Indeed, the promise of free land drew hundreds of thousands of land-hungry people from not only the United States but also Europe. When the bill became law, House Speaker Galusha Grow acknowledged the role of Greeley and his paper: "Its friends are more indebted for success to the unwavering support given it by the New York *Tribune* than to aught else."[62] But even before the dream of a free homestead became a reality, Horace Greeley realized that the spread of slavery into the territory threatened to undermine any benefit it might offer to free labor. While he worked for land reform, he also struggled to keep slavery from spreading into the territories and making them unfit for free settlers.

4

BATTLING SLAVERY
IN THE EXPANDING WEST

No newspaper journalist in the
nineteenth century, perhaps,
has exerted a wider and more
powerful influence upon
the people of this country
than has the editor of the
New York Tribune.

William Lloyd Garrison, 1864

We deny the authority of Congress,
of a territorial legislature, or of
any individuals to give legal
existence to slavery in any
territory in the United States.

Republican Party platform, 1860

Slavery was a great moral evil to Horace Greeley and to many of the reformers of his day. His fight to contain the system, however, went beyond his sense of right and wrong. He did not believe that slavery and free labor could coexist in the same area. If southerners spread their "peculiar institution" into the western lands, those lands, so important to his solution for urban poverty, would be unfit for the settlement of free labor. Other political and personal motives influenced his opposition to slavery's expansion, but the availability of land for free labor was primary.

Greeley brought powerful weapons to the battle. His first, and most effective, was the *New York Weekly Tribune,* with two hundred thousand copies in the hands of western farmers each week. Next, he used his political connections. Having served a short term in Congress himself, Greeley maintained close ties with several congressmen. He was also a founder and leader of the Republican Party and left his imprint on the platforms of 1856 and 1860. Finally, although a self-proclaimed poor public speaker, his speeches on the promise of the West, the evils of slavery, and the truth of Republican politics always attracted large crowds. He used every means at his disposal to fight slavery's extension into the western territories.

Greeley's first experience with slavery came at age fifteen in Poultney, Vermont. A young runaway slave was working in Poultney when his owner found him and attempted to forcibly return him to servitude. The villagers arose, whisked the runaway to safety, and forced the owner to return home empty-handed. Greeley recalled that the people had not acted because of hatred of the South, but from hatred of injustice and oppression.[1]

After he moved to New York, formed the political triumvirate with Thurlow Weed and William Seward, and started the *Tribune,* Greeley's views on the effects of slavery on the nation expanded. By this time he had also begun to visualize the West as a haven for New York City's poor. He believed the voracious appetite of slave owners for new land could drag the country into war. He also ascribed to the conventional wisdom that democracy worked only when the country remained compact and the citizens maintained direct contact with their representatives. So he fought the development of the Oregon Territory and the annexation of Texas. Ultimately, his aspirations for the nation, his political party, and his plan to relieve poverty in the cities and people the West came together in the fight to keep slavery out of Kansas. From the day Illinois senator Stephen A. Douglas introduced the Kansas–Nebraska bill in 1854 until Kansas became a state in 1861, the fight against the spread of slavery into that territory was seldom off the pages of the *Tribune.*

But before Greeley's vision of the safety valve expanded to include all the West, he opposed plans to bring Oregon into the United States, arguing that settlement in such remote regions would undermine America's democratic institutions. The area was too far away to allow effective government or to develop that "deep sympathy," "attachment," and "intimate knowledge" needed for the stability and growth of republican institutions.[2] After Democrat James K. Polk used the platform of "the reoccupation of Oregon and the reannexation of Texas" to defeat Greeley's political idol Henry Clay for the presidency in 1844, the editorials against acquisition of Oregon became more strident. According to Greeley, a vote for Oregon became a vote for slavery in Texas.[3]

On the question of bringing Texas into the Union, Greeley was also an early and ardent foe. For him, Texas held all the dangers of Oregon, plus it was slave territory. He considered it "incredible" that any sane person would support annexation. Such action, he believed, would not only fuel a bitter controversy with England and France but also renew the intersectional battle over the extension of slavery. He vowed to oppose the measure with untiring determination.[4] The annexation of Texas, Greeley warned, would not only strengthen slavery in that state and in the nation but also cause "indignation and alarm" in "all Christendom." The result would be a revival of friction and hostility between the North and South over the slavery issue, a controversy he believed all reasonable people opposed.[5]

As the annexation moved closer to reality, Greeley added other reasons to his argument against acquiring the new territory. He especially stressed the likelihood of war with Mexico and the moral and financial cost of such a war. It would increase the public debt and create an army and navy that the country had no other need for except to make war. He warned that making war on a peaceful nation would expose the United States to the world as a "crafty, grasping and unprincipled Nation." If the conflict led to bloodshed, he believed that Mexico would be less to blame than "those of us who have not resisted with all our might the perfidious act of rapine which is the cause of this most unnatural drama of murder."[6] Despite his impassioned words, John Tyler used the expansionist sentiment expressed in Polk's election to push the annexation bill through Congress in February 1845, just before the new president's inauguration.

After Texas became the twenty-eighth state on 29 December 1845, Greeley seemed to accept the fact and stated that he held no unkind feelings toward the new state, but vowed to continued his battle against slavery there. He also promised to fight any move to carve additional slave states from Texas. But for the present, he was willing to wait to see if any good came from the addition of Texas to the Union.[7]

When admission of the newest slave state aroused the war spirit in Mexico, Greeley returned to the attack and administration leaders again became his targets. As Polk dispatched General Zachary Taylor toward the Rio Grande, the editor considered the United States government "utterly wrong" to threaten war with Mexico over the disputed territory. He acknowledged that the American army could easily defeat the army of Mexico, but warned that the nation could accrue no honor or benefit for an unjust war. Killing Mexicans and taking their territory was "murder," according to Greeley. He called for Americans to "awake and arrest the work of butchery ere it shall be too late to preserve your souls from the guilt of wholesale slaughter."[8]

Few people doubted that the war with Mexico would add a large portion to the United States' western lands. On 12 May 1846, the day following Polk's plea for Congress to declare war, Greeley railed against extending the American empire by the sword and praised House passage, in August 1846, of the Wilmot Proviso, which prohibited slavery in any land acquired during the war with Mexico.[9]

Throughout the conflict he fought the acquisition of Mexican territory as the spoils of war. He declared that although California should be an independent nation, the American government was "bent on `liberating' the Californians from themselves." He also argued that the United States would benefit more by improving the territory the country already possessed than by "scheming and fighting for more."[10]

Manifest Destiny, however, ran roughshod over Greeley's reasoning. The Treaty of Guadalupe Hidalgo on 2 February 1848 ended the war and added half a million square miles of Mexico's finest land, including the cherished coast of California, to the United States. As Greeley had predicted in 1844, the addition of this huge block of new land added tinder to the slavery controversy. Fear that several new slave states would form from the newly acquired territory aroused northerners. In the meantime, the rise of the Free-Soil Party and an anti-slavery faction of the Democratic Party in the North confirmed the fears of southern extremists and made them more adamant in defending their institution.

Besides his editorials in the *Tribune*, Greeley used his considerable political clout as a power in the Whig Party to fight the extension of slavery into the territories. He carried his battle to Washington during his brief term in Congress in 1848, fighting slavery whenever possible. By the end of the session in December 1848, emotions were aflame in Congress and in the nation and there was little doubt that there would soon be open conflict.

The discovery of gold in California that year helped to force the showdown over the question of slavery in the newly acquired territory. Only the near-superhuman effort of a dying Henry Clay quieted the sectional hostilities with the Compromise of 1850—a group of measures that brought California into the Union as a free state, settled the New Mexico–Texas border dispute, organized the New Mexico and Utah Territories with the provision that their citizens would decide the slavery question when the territories became states, and passed a strict fugitive slave act. Clay's last great effort seemed to have calmed the troubled waters.

Battling Slavery

But the peace was merely a respite. Stephen Douglas, who worked so hard to help Clay bring the peace, destroyed it almost singlehandedly in 1854. On 4 December 1853, Iowa Senator A. C. Dodge introduced a bill to organize the Nebraska Territory for statehood. The bill moved to the Committee on Territories, where Chairman Douglas adopted it as his own. Douglas's and the nation's interest in a transcontinental railroad had grown throughout the late 1840s and early 1850s, while sectional competition for a favorable route kept pace. A line that would tie either the North or the South to the West promised to assure the predominance of either freedom or slavery in that region. Douglas wanted to secure a central or northern railway to the advantage of his state, his section, and himself. Native Americans, with land titles ensured by federal treaty, stood between him and the railroad, which would need clear title to the land and enough potential customers to make the investment pay. The Illinois senator decided the most direct path to his goal was to prepare the Nebraska Territory, which stood between his state and a central route to the West, for statehood. This would not only allow the federal government to renegotiate the treaties and move Native Americans away from the projected route but also attract more customers for the proposed railroad.

Extending statehood to the western regions, however, faced greater obstacles than relocating people with no political power and nothing to protect them but pieces of paper. The admission of California as a free state under the Compromise of 1850 had given the free states a sixteen-to-fifteen edge in the Senate. Oregon, Washington, New Mexico, Utah, and Minnesota loomed on the horizon as possible additions to the northern advantage. Because the Nebraska Territory lay north of 36 degrees 30 minutes (the line across the western

lands established by the Missouri Compromise of 1820 to separate future slave and free states), the new state would further
increase the free-state margin. Furthermore, the territory abut-
ted Missouri's western border and, with Iowa on the north and
Illinois to the east, threatened to surround Missouri slave owners on three sides with free states. Yet without southern support
for Nebraska statehood, Douglas's efforts were hopeless.

The bill that emerged from Douglas's Committee on Territories on 4 January 1854 reflected his attempt to garner southern favor. The revised measure included several amendments
and a discourse on the status of slavery in the federal lands.
Douglas explained that the Compromise of 1850 had negated
Congress's role in controlling slavery in the territories and
had established the precedent of "popular sovereignty." This
ploy, he hoped, would avoid a fight over the extension of slavery into the territories. Unfortunately, he badly misjudged
sentiments in both the North and South.

First, southern congressmen immediately recognized
Douglas's bill as an opportunity to rid themselves of the odi-
ous Missouri Compromise. Second, they wanted Congress
specifically to relinquish control over slavery in the territories. Finally, the southerners wanted Douglas to divide the
Nebraska Territory into two potential states, one free and one
slave, thereby maintaining the balance in the Senate. *This* was
the asking price of southern support.

Douglas agreed to pay. He asked the *Washington Sentinel*
to reprint his bill, explaining that the last section had been
omitted through clerical error. Appearing on 10 January 1854,
this added section claimed that the bill meant to carry out three
principles of the Compromise of 1850: slave owners could recover their "property" in the territories as well as in the states,
the Supreme Court held final authority on personal freedom

and ownership of slaves, and the citizens in the territories and new states had the right to decide all questions on slavery there. Douglas's addition would repeal the Missouri Compromise and replace it with the principle of popular sovereignty.

The reaction from the North was immediate and fervent. Rumor of the impending changes reached Horace Greeley and he responded on the same day as the revised *Sentinel* article appeared. The editor expressed disbelief that any conscientious person who had professed conviction in the idea of human freedom could so easily abandon that principle.[11] He later acknowledged that he began his fight against the spread of slavery into Kansas on that day, a fight to which he gave all his strength.[12]

Historian Allan Nevins captured the essence of the times when he described the national scene soon after Douglas had reported his bill out of committee: "Dark stormclouds hung over" the entire country, "and livid lightning shook a portentous finger across the recently smiling landscape."[13] The bill rekindled northern fears of southern plots to create more slave states in the western plains, seize Cuba, and reopen the slave trade. The claim that the Compromise of 1850 had in effect repealed the Missouri Compromise was a blow to those northerners who had supported the recent attempt at conciliation. Greeley suggested a popular movement to compel Congress to repeal the so-called repudiating clause in the 1850 laws.[14]

Despite Greeley's efforts in the press and William Seward's and other antislavery members' fight in Congress, the bill passed the House of Representatives 113 to 100 and the Senate by a margin of 37 to 14. The vote in both houses reflected sectional, rather than party, lines. Northern Whigs, Free-Soilers, and Free-Soil northern Democrats opposed the measure. Southern Whigs and Democrats supported Douglas's bill. President Franklin Pierce immediately signed it into law.

Greeley quickly saw the major defect in Douglas's argument for popular sovereignty. Everything depended upon the laws in effect in the territories before settlement. The person who spoke of settlers creating their own laws and own constitution without taking into account the existing territorial regulations was a "dissembler" who walked "in craftiness" and laid "in wait to deceive."[15] Douglas's failure to fully explain popular sovereignty or define at what stage in the process voters could exclude slavery created an atmosphere of uncertainty and the likelihood that both the North and the South would try to influence the outcome of any election.

On 26 April 1854, even before the bill became law, Eli Thayer incorporated the Massachusetts Emigrant Aid Society to encourage settlers to move to Kansas and to raise money to finance their move. Thayer envisioned a venture that would both fight slavery and make a profit. While transporting Free-Soil settlers to Kansas, the society would build towns, mills, schools, and churches to serve them after they arrived. Greeley joined Thayer's drive to raise $5 million in stock subscriptions to begin the enterprise and used his pen to encourage settlers to move to Kansas and make it first a free territory, then a free state. He later acknowledged he did everything he could to inspire "capable, energetic, independent farmers and mechanics" to emigrate to Kansas.[16] Although the Emigrant Aid Society sent only 1,240 settlers to the territory between 1854 and 1855, the effect the movement had on the minds of southerners far outweighed its meager accomplishments. To further exacerbate emotions in the South, Amos A. Lawrence, Dr. Charles Robinson, and Samuel C. Pomeroy, all officers or agents of the Emigrant Aid Society, became the leaders of the Free-Soil movement in Kansas.[17]

The slave states, meanwhile, were not to be outdone. Missouri, with its slaves concentrated along its western border

Battling Slavery

with Kansas, had a vested interest in the territory's future. Hundreds of Missourians slipped across the border and staked claim to the best acreage in Kansas, even before the land became legally available. Southerners, too, had their societies, with names like Blue Lodges, Social Bands, and Sons of the South, dedicated to protecting their "property" rights in Kansas. Northerners claimed these groups began forming in 1850 with the expressed purpose of "stealing Kansas." Southerners countered that they organized these lodges to counteract Thayer's "rowdies and vagabonds," who were arriving in Kansas with a Bible in one hand and a rifle in the other.[18] Proslavery newspapers also joined the fray. The *Frontier News* in Westport, Kansas, for example, called out to the "Freemen of the South" and "Pioneers of the West" to halt the march of Greeley and Thayer's "abolitionist tyrants" into the Missouri Valley, before they ruined that "hesperidean garden" and destroyed "the whole institution of slavery."[19]

The first test of popular sovereignty in Kansas came in the fall of 1854. President Pierce named Andrew H. Reeder, a Pennsylvania lawyer, as the first territorial governor. His initial task was to oversee the election of a legislature in November. Shortly after arriving at his post, Reeder estimated that there were between fifteen hundred and two thousand eligible voters in the territory. On election day, 2,871 voters cast ballots. Missourians had followed the exhortations of their proslavery Democratic senator David R. Atchison, who a few weeks earlier had told them that their peace, quiet, and property depended upon their willingness to send five hundred young men into Kansas to vote in favor of slavery. According to one later estimate, Missourians crossed the border and cast more than seventeen hundred illegal votes. The legislature thus elected was overwhelmingly proslavery.[20]

For Greeley, with the slave owners in Missouri's six westernmost counties holding slaves valued in the millions of dollars, the election's results were predictable. He reasoned that it was unrealistic to expect an imaginary line to prevent the proslavery forces from seeking to preserve their self-interests. Only the "willfully blind or deplorably stupid" could not have foreseen such results from the destruction of the Missouri Compromise. He hoped "stimulated free immigration" eventually would carry the state for freedom; but for the present, "bold, bad men," who were basking in their success, had secured Kansas for slavery.[21]

The Free-Soil settlers reacted to the fraudulent election by calling their own convention at Topeka. The Topeka gathering formed a separate government with an antislavery constitution. From this point the rival factions, neither of which could legitimately claim to represent the people of Kansas, vied for federal recognition as the true territorial government. As historian Kenneth Stampp has suggested, if President Franklin Pierce had disavowed both claims and called for a new, better supervised election, he could possibly have averted the bloodshed that followed in 1856.[22]

Greeley, meanwhile, continued his efforts to "stimulate" immigration to wrest Kansas from the grasp of slaveholders.[23] As violence increased in the territory, he worked to strengthen Free-Soil resolve: "Let there be no bolting, no flinching, no weak recoiling." He encouraged brave men, whom neither self-interest nor threat of violence could divert from their purpose, to emigrate to Kansas. For such men he promised a land filled with nature's bounties, including a healthy climate and fertile soil—the most delightful and inviting land to be found in all the "unoccupied domain."[24]

Though Greeley usually supported his arguments with rea-

Battling Slavery

son, he sometimes resorted to name calling and appeal to the baser emotions. He seldom addressed the Missourians as other than tobacco-chewing, whiskey-drinking, "Border Ruffians." This "rabble," who had crossed into Kansas in numbers sufficient to overpower the legitimate voters, "were of the lowest grade of whites that can be found in a slave country, and all know that such are the most degraded class of mortals," he wrote in one especially inflammatory editorial.[25] Later, in a very un-Greeley call for violence, he proclaimed Sharp's rifles as the "true peacemakers" when one had to deal with the "border ruffians." Greeley even published an appeal from John Brown for funds nearly a year after Brown had massacred five proslavery settlers at Pottawatomie, Kansas Territory.[26] Such fanning of the flames did nothing to bring peace to Kansas.

Greeley also urged Congress to fight for a free Kansas. After proslavery forces had won the first legislative election, he avowed the free states' steadfast determination that Kansas would never come into the Union as a slave state. He exhorted the new Congress not to grant this "impudent farce" of an election any shadow of respectability.[27] Just before the fall national elections in 1855, Greeley advised voters to defeat any congressmen who supported the repeal of the Missouri Compromise and to instruct those elected to seat the delegate from the extralegal Topeka "legislature," instead of the "pretender" the Missourians had selected.[28]

Meanwhile, the fight over slavery's extension into the territories was having a profound effect on party politics. The furor that erupted over the Kansas–Nebraska Act led to the split of the Democrats, the demise of the Whigs, and the birth of the Republican Party. Greeley, calling the passage of the bill the "death-blow" to northern complacency, immediately began working to mold the anti-Nebraska forces into a new party. He later described the sentiment for a new antislavery party as a spontaneous movement that began in the West and quickly spread across all the free states by the end of 1854.[29]

At the forefront of the drive, Greeley was one of the "moving spirits" behind a convention that met at Saratoga, New York, on 16 August 1854, barely ten weeks after the hated Kansas–Nebraska Act became law. As chairman of the convention's platform committee, he help to create a document that avoided divisive issues while strongly opposing the extension of slavery and the Kansas–Nebraska Act. The usually blunt and unbending Greeley showed considerable political adeptness by leading the various anti-Nebraska factions to a common stand against slavery's spread into the territory. The Saratoga platform also encouraged northern settlers to move to Kansas to win the state for the Free-Soil cause.

The Republican Party's position on slavery, Greeley explained, was "defensive, not aggressive": the party sought to preserve freedom, not destroy slavery. He depicted the birth of the new party as a "glorious beginning," not the ending of an era. Indeed, he believed that slavery should and would disappear from the country; but the immediate task was to stop the system's growth and extension into the territories.[30] These ideas came to represent the official Republican Party position on the subject. Greeley served on the platform committees at the national conventions in 1856 and 1860 and helped write the planks that committed the party to the fight against slavery's extension.[31] In 1856 he published a political tract on the extension of slavery and included details on the Wilmot Proviso, the Compromise of 1850, and the Kansas–Nebraska struggle. He also produced a similar tract that included much of the same information and added the proposed Kansas constitutions, important speeches on the subject, and specifics on the Homestead Bill.

In Kansas, meanwhile, the proslavery interests used political machinations, gerrymandering, intimidation, and outright fraud to maintain control of the legislature despite the ever-increasing preponderance of Free-Soil settlers. But the ruling minority was fighting a losing battle. In January 1857 Greeley proclaimed that people across the North believed that Kansas soon would join the Union as a free state.[32] Few nonpartisan observers (if such could have been found) would have disagreed. The availability of good land at low prices had attracted thousands of Free-Soil settlers. Some of the new citizens were from New England, some from New York, but most were from farms closer to the Mississippi River. They had come not as abolitionists to fight slavery but as farmers seeking an opportunity to improve their own lives. They supported free soil in Kansas primarily because they did not want to compete with slave labor. Historian Allan Nevins later noted, "Kansas was not the daughter of New England, but of the Ohio Valley."[33]

Although the Free-Soil population had grown to a clear majority by 1857, the Kansas proslavery element had one last hurrah. A convention, composed of sixty delegates selected in an election controlled by the proslavery minority, met in Lecompton to created a constitution to present to Congress in a bid for statehood. Nevins described the constitutional delegates as "ignorant, semi-illiterate, and prejudiced men, totally unrepresentative of the Kansas population."[34] The document they produced reflected their unique qualifications. The Lecompton Constitution legalized the owning, buying, selling, and importation of slaves in Kansas; prohibited the state legislature from emancipating slaves without the owners' consent; reinforced the Fugitive Slave Law; and barred free blacks from entering the state. To guard against immediate changes to this proslavery provision should the Free-Soilers gain power, the constitution forbade amendment before 1864. The convention also selected its president, John Calhoun, to head an interim government, replacing the federally appointed governor and newly elected territorial legislature. Calhoun also had to validate all election results until the state government was in office. Although frontier democracy seldom lived up to Frederick Jackson Turner's projections, the Lecompton delegates behaved badly even by frontier standards.[35]

Knowing there was little chance that Congress would accept such a document without its ratification by a majority of the state's voters, the convention very adroitly confronted this hurdle. Because the article on slavery was the controversial portion of the constitution, according to its creators, the state's voters only needed to vote on that article, not the entire document. So in a special referendum on 21 December 1857, Kansas voters could choose the constitution "with slavery" or "without slavery." If the voters selected "without slavery," the constitution still protected the property rights of slave owners who already had slaves in the state. This left the door open for a myriad of abuses. Horace Greeley naturally condemned the Lecompton convention and its handiwork as "bogus" and urged the territory's Free-Soil majority to boycott the election.[36] Despite this obvious attempt by a fraudulent convention selected by a minority of citizens to force a repulsive constitution on the majority of Kansans, Democratic president James Buchanan called the arrangement "fair" and urged the voters to go to the polls in December and express their choice. On 21 December Free-Soilers stayed at home, and the constitution "with slavery" passed, 6,226 to 569.

Antislavery forces, meanwhile, had won a majority of seats in the new territorial legislature that would convene in 1858, unless Calhoun's interim government replaced them and the governor. Free-Soil leaders convinced acting governor Frederick P. Stanton to call a special session of the new legislature for 7 December 1857. Although acting without legal authority, as their term did not begin until after the New Year, the legislators passed an act calling for a special referendum to vote on the entire Lecompton Constitution. In that election, on 4 January 1858, 10,226 voters rejected the document, 138 accepted it "without slavery," and 23 accepted it "with slavery."[37]

Obviously, most Kansans did not support the Lecompton Constitution. Yet President Buchanan urged Congress to accept the results of the December 21 election and admit Kansas into the Union.[38] After Buchanan announced his support of the Lecompton document, Greeley labeled him a "Border Ruffian ex-officio." In an attempt to make political hay of the Kansas debacle, Greeley even attacked Robert J. Walker. (Buchanan had persuaded Walker to accept the governorship of Kansas by promising the administration's full support for fair elections, then apparently abandoned him when he tried to carry out these instructions.)[39]

The battle against the Lecompton Constitution also led ardent Republican Greeley into an unusual political alliance with Democrat Douglas, one of the "bold, bad men" who had worked for the repeal of the Missouri Compromise.[40] Douglas, appalled by the corruption of popular sovereignty in Kansas, opposed the Lecompton document and chastised President Buchanan for supporting it. Greeley, eager to defeat the "bogus" constitution and exploit the rift in the Democratic leadership, sprang to Douglas's side.

Douglas determined to delay the congressional vote on Kansas statehood as long as possible in order to allow public opposition to grow. William Seward and the Republicans in Congress joined Douglas, northern Democrats, and the Know-

Nothing Party to force the delay. Greeley, meanwhile, used his newspaper to build voter resistance to Kansas statehood under the Lecompton Constitution. He attacked the document and its backers while promising political support for all opponents, no matter their party. Republican and *Tribune* praise for Douglas became so strong that many considered him the party's likely candidate in the 1860 presidential election.

Greeley's tactics found favor in the Northeast but did not appeal to Illinois Republicans, who hoped to defeat Douglas and elect Abraham Lincoln to the Senate in fall of 1858. Lincoln wrote to Illinois' Republican senator Lyman Trumbull asking why the *Tribune* praised Douglas and if Washington Republicans had decided that the party could best be served by sacrificing its members in Illinois. Lincoln then warned that if the *Tribune* continued extolling Douglas's virtues to its five to ten thousand Republican readers in the state, some would be swayed to vote for the Democrat.[41]

Greeley later explained that he understood why the Illinois Republicans had opposed Douglas. He had been in office for many years and they felt that they finally had a chance to defeat him. They also portrayed him as an unprincipled politician who only condemned the Lecompton Constitution because it was politically expedient. "They believed, therefore, that consistency and fidelity to principle required them to resist his reelection."[42] Greeley claimed that he, on the other hand, considered himself above party politics. He joined with Douglas and other Democrats who helped Free-Soil forces defeat slavery and the Lecompton Constitution.[43]

Greeley had reason to maintain the wisdom of his position, even though his stand had cost him subscriptions in Illinois. Although the Lecompton Constitution carried in the Senate by a vote of thirty-three to twenty-five, it did not slip through

Battling Slavery

the House. By 1 April 1858, when the measure came before the House of Representatives, the public outcry had convinced northern Democrats that a vote for the constitution as it stood would be political suicide. The chamber added an amendment requiring a popular vote on the entire constitution. The Senate rejected the change. Indiana senator William H. English broke the deadlock with another amendment that would allow the people of Kansas to vote on the entire constitution. If they accepted it, they would immediately acquire statehood, the standard federal land grant of 3,988,868 acres, and a bonus of 5 percent of the net proceeds from an upcoming government sale of 2 million acres of public land. A rejection of the constitution meant Kansas would have to wait until the population grew large enough to become a congressional district, which would probably take at least two more years. No matter that the amendment seemed to offer a bribe for acceptance of the Lecompton Constitution, the Free-Soil settlers in Kansas would have the opportunity to vote on the entire document. Both chambers of Congress quickly approved this unequal compromise, despite Douglas and Seward's opposition.[44]

Greeley expressed the opinion of many of his readers when he called the English amendment a "vicious blunderbuss" that would "kick over" those who supported it. He also added that he was not distraught that the measure had passed because he knew that Kansas voters would quickly reject the Lecompton Constitution.[45] His prediction was accurate; Kansas voters overwhelmingly rejected the hated document, 11,812 to 1,926, even though this meant they would have to wait to join the Union.[46] Thus ended the battle over slavery in Kansas. The battle that would end slavery in the other territories would begin in earnest in less than three years. Greeley's editorials aroused public opinion, which helped to win the first battle; but his acrimonious words also helped to polarize the country and lead to the second one.

In 1859, the year after Kansans had rejected the Lecompton Constitution, Greeley traveled across the territory on his way to California. He spoke at gatherings along the way, enlightening his listeners on Republican Party principles. He also explained the differences between "true" democracy and "squatter sovereignty" to a convention of nearly one thousand voters who were meeting at Osawatomie to decide the future of Kansas and the Republican Party in the territory.[47] Greeley spoke at Topeka, Lawrence, Prairie City, and any other town where the stage stopped long enough for a crowd to gather. And the crowds did gather, for the people in Kansas knew and loved Horace Greeley. So much so that when the territory became a state it included Greeley County and the towns of Horace and Tribune to honor him for his contributions to Kansas.

Greeley fought the extension of slavery into the western territories and especially into Kansas for many reasons, some moral, some political, and some practical. His desire to keep the region fit for the settlement of free labor was a primary motivation. He hoped that New York City's poor would move to farms in Kansas, but such was not the case. He did inspire new settlers; but they came from the Ohio Valley, not from New York City. Still, Greeley's editorials helped shape public opinion and win support for the Free-Soil cause among northern voters, and his efforts to organize the Republican Party and place that party on record in opposition to slavery's extension was important in keeping the West open for Free-Soil settlers. Furthermore, during the crucial struggle against the Lecompton Constitution in 1858, he helped arouse northern voter opposition, ensuring the hated document's defeat. He was not the only foe of slavery's extension into the territories, but his words reached more readers' eyes than those of any other American writer of his time. Meanwhile, as he fought against the extension of slavery into the West, he worked with equal fervor for a railroad that would bring settlers to this region and carry their produce back to the eastern markets.

5
FIGHTING
FOR THE RAILROAD WEST

Viewed in retrospect, it is apparent that, for good or ill, it was chiefly railroad companies that promoted the West, facilitated the migration of great numbers of settlers from home and abroad, and were the first to penetrate and spearhead settlement in the plains country.

Oscar Osburn Winther,
The Transportation Frontier

RESOLVED: *That we, the delegated representatives of the Republican electors of the United States, in convention assembled, in discharge of the duty we owe to our constituents and our country, unite in the following declarations: ... 16. That a railroad to the Pacific Ocean is imperatively demanded by the interests of the whole country; that the federal government ought to render immediate and efficient aid in its construction.*

Republican Party platform, 1860

93

Although no one apparently knows who first suggested a transcontinental railroad in the United States, Horace Greeley was an early proponent. Reflecting on the question in 1868, he recalled that the mad rush to California after the discovery of gold in 1848 had convinced him that the construction of a railway from the Missouri River to the Pacific Ocean was "imperative and inevitable."[1] More than three decades earlier, however, even before the United States had its first mile of track, Robert Mills had proposed a line from the headwaters of the Mississippi to the Oregon Territory. When Dr. Hartwell Carver recommended to Congress in 1832 that the federal government build a railroad from New York City to San Francisco, there were only 140 miles of track in the entire country.[2] Still, the idea of connecting the industrial and commercial centers of the East with the Pacific Coast ports by rail did not begin to gain credence until the mid-1840s, when New York merchant Asa Whitney undertook his campaign. Whitney had been in China in 1843, when the emperor opened the first ports to free trade. The vision of China as a vast market captivated him. John C. Frémont later described the Oriental trade route as "the golden vein which runs through history" and assured Americans that it would permanently follow the railroad across the United States to San Francisco.[3] For the next ten years, from the mid-1840s to the mid-1850s, Whitney traveled extensively, visiting nearly every state, advocating the construction of a transcontinental railroad.[4]

Fighting for the Railroad

He realized that lack of surplus capital in the West meant that eastern financiers would have to fund the scheme, and eastern financial backing depended upon federal support. In January 1845 he presented his plan to Congress for a railroad from the Great Lakes to the Oregon coast. He asked for a land grant sixty miles wide along the route, the sale of which would finance construction. Most congressmen, believing the request excessive and the project impractical, readily dismissed Whitney's plan.

One person who took Whitney seriously was Horace Greeley. As a staunch supporter of Henry Clay's "American System," which included internal improvements, he believed that an efficient transportation network was necessary for the country's growth. He favored clearing the navigable rivers, building new harbors, and constructing a "national road." In keeping with his theme of western opportunity for the eastern poor, he reasoned that if the federal government diverted half the navy's annual $9 million budget from that "thriftless abyss" to building a transportation system, there would be more jobs at higher wages, westerners would receive more for their produce and pay less for eastern goods, and the entire nation would benefit.[5]

So naturally Greeley applauded this "magnificent project." He agreed with Whitney's claim that the railroad would expand trade with China, Japan, the rest of Asia, and the Pacific islands.[6] But to the reformer in Greeley, the land sales to finance the railroad offered additional opportunities. If Congress restricted the land purchases to no more than 160 acres, society's benefits, including schools, churches, roads, and industry, would spread more quickly and evenly than if speculators bought large tracts and held them while awaiting higher prices. He believed that such a restriction would help to settle the land quickly and guarantee the success of the railroad venture.[7]

Another benefit of a transcontinental railroad, according to Greeley, would be an improvement in the traveling conditions and reduction in the time and cost of an overland journey to California. Such improvement would accelerate the migration of "intelligent, capable, virtuous" women to that state. An 1852 census counted only 22,193 females in California's population of 264,435, a disproportion, Greeley lamented, that caused great degradation in the public morals. Yet with California wages for women being three times as high as those in New York, Greeley believed that the railroad would encourage tens of thousands of women to move to the Golden State each year. This migration would benefit California, the country, the women themselves, and the railroad.[8]

Horace Greeley also reasoned that a railroad would not only open the West for settlement but also bind the country together. With the migration to Oregon and California, he, like many others, doubted if democracy could survive in such a fragmented country. He doubted that western citizens, with fifteen hundred miles of "desert" and two "great mountain-chains" separating them from the rest of the country, could effectively participate in the national government. The easiest journey from the West Coast to Washington, D.C. was several thousand miles by boat and a fifty-mile trek through the disease-ridden jungles of Panama.[9] To Greeley, there was only one answer: a Pacific railroad. He later avowed, "I am now and always for the Pacific railroad at all hazards and unconditionally." Even when others scoffed and compared a transcontinental railroad to a "tunnel under the Atlantic or a bridge to the moon," Greeley claimed to have concerned himself only with plans for turning the dream into a reality.[10]

As part of his fight for an improved national transportation system, Greeley attended the River and Harbor Conven-

Fighting for the Railroad

tion in Chicago in July 1847. Called to protest President James K. Polk's veto of a river and harbor bill, the gathering attracted twenty-three hundred people from eighteen states, including Illinois' new congressman, Abraham Lincoln. Greeley covered the convention for the *Tribune*. After the formal meeting ended, he assumed the role of chairman and led the group in adopting a resolution supporting a transcontinental railroad over the central route.[11]

President James K. Polk's December 1848 state of the union address confirming a large gold strike in California gave railroad supporters more ammunition for their fight. Editorials justifying federal support for the railroad soon became more common in the *Tribune*. Greeley argued that the transcontinental railroad would not only allow the United States to control the wealth coming from California's gold but also open the vast area between the Mississippi River and the Pacific Ocean to settlement. This, in turn, would add more wealth to the United States than the opening of the East India trade had brought Great Britain. Therefore, because the entire country would derive great benefit from the railroad, the national government should finance the undertaking.[12]

Federal aid for a transcontinental railroad came closer to a reality in 1850, when Senator Stephen A. Douglas of Illinois sought financing for a railroad to connect Chicago with Cairo at the southern tip of the state. He proposed a land grant similar to those Congress had given western canal developers. The Wabash and Erie Canal, for example, had received a grant of alternate 640-acre sections of federal land along the right-of-way. To garner support from southerners, the Illinois railroad would join at Cairo with another stretching to Mobile, Alabama. Douglas's machinations succeeded. Congress granted Illinois, Mississippi, and Alabama the right-of-way for a railroad from Chicago and Galena, Illinois, to Mobile, plus alternate sections within six miles on each side of the railroad. This act in May 1850 set the precedent for the 1862 act in which the federal government voted to use its public lands to finance a railroad connecting the eastern half of the nation with its western coast.

While Douglas's north–south railroad helped to bind the rival sections of the country together, the struggle over a route for an east–west railroad helped pull them apart. The Compromise of 1850 patched up the sectional differences enough to allow Secretary of War Jefferson Davis to include two hundred thousand dollars for a survey of the most practical and economical route for a railroad to the Pacific in his Army Appropriation Bill in March 1853. Engineers surveyed four possible alternatives. Isaac I. Steven, Washington's new territorial governor, explored the route from Saint Paul to Seattle between the forty-seventh and forty-ninth parallels. Captain John W. Gunnison followed the thirty-eighth parallel along the Chicago–St. Louis–San Francisco route, and Lieutenant Amiel W. Whipple checked the Memphis–San Francisco route along the thirty-fifth parallel. A Major Emory led an expedition from New Orleans to San Diego along the thirty-second parallel.[13]

Although Greeley preferred the northern or central routes, he advocated conciliation. While Congress debated the survey amendment to the appropriations bill, he proclaimed that the "unity and dignity of the Republic, and the convenience of the people" demanded a railroad to the Pacific. He then offered to support any "tolerable" plan that would ensure the railroad's completion within a reasonable time.[14] After an extensive survey, the engineers reported to Congress that all four routes were practical.

Throughout the 1850s Greeley used the power of his press to win public support for a railroad to the Pacific and to call

Fighting for the Railroad

for men of action to complete the undertaking within their lifetime. There would still be an abundance of important work left for the next generation, he wrote.[15] He later added that a railroad connecting the states east of the Mississippi with "our new empire" was among the most urgent needs of the time and its importance, "Politically, Socially, [and] Commercially," could not be overestimated. Although he still did not publicly advocate a specific route, he ridiculed the Gadsden Purchase, which cleared the way for the southern route.[16]

Meanwhile, Stephen Douglas's effort to remove the obstacles hindering the central route destroyed the Compromise of 1850, helped to bring on the Civil War, and delayed a federal bill for support of a transcontinental railroad until after the South had seceded. In an attempt to clear the way for a route that would be in the best interests of his state and himself, Douglas brought forth a measure to organize the Nebraska Territory for statehood. His Kansas–Nebraska Act of 1854 created two states and allowed the people living in them to decide the issue of slavery for themselves. The act rekindled the fires of sectionalism and destroyed the veneer of cooperation created by the Compromise of 1850, virtually assuring that there would be no Pacific railroad until the country confronted the issue of slavery.

The passing of the Kansas–Nebraska Act on 22 May 1854 and President Franklin Pierce's signing it into law had prompted Horace Greeley to call for northern antislavery men to unite and support the emigration of Free-Soil men to Kansas.[17] Outrage over the law moved its opponents to create a new political party to resist the extension of slavery into the territories. When the party met to select John C. Frémont as its presidential candidate in 1856, Greeley was on the platform committee. He had realized the political importance of the transcontinental railroad as early as April 1853, when he wrote his friend Congressman Schuyler Colfax that in the 1856 election he would support anyone who was "thoroughly and heartily" for the Pacific railroad.[18] Indeed, at the 1856 convention he included a plank in the Republican platform that committed the party to the undertaking.

The Republicans lost that election; but Greeley continued his fight for the "grandest enterprise of the age." He argued that the increased value of the property along the route would more than offset the cost of construction. Additionally, he predicted that emigration from the Atlantic and Mississippi Valley states to California would quadruple. Even if the railroad cost the country $100 million, he proclaimed that it would benefit the country and its people more than a "hundred Buena Vistas" (referring to a victory in the recent war with Mexico). While southerners and their sympathizers clamored for Cuba or the rest of Mexico as new territory in which to extend slavery, Greeley recommended the railroad as a moral alternative. He asserted that the line would not only strengthen the nation by binding the East and West together but also divert the nation's energy from "filibustering and Annexation forays."[19]

While fighting for the railroad in the *Tribune*, Greeley continued the political struggle behind the scenes with letters to Congress—especially to Congressman Colfax. Greeley urged his friend to introduce a bill that offered a small amount of cash and a mile-wide strip of public land to the company that would build a railroad along any route between the Mississippi River and the Pacific Ocean. The editor also suggested attaching the measure as an amendment to a less controversial bill.[20] Perhaps an amendment to another measure might pass where a separate railroad bill would not. This ploy did not work either, as the fight between northern and southern

Fighting for the Railroad

congressmen over the route continued to block the Pacific Railroad.

Greeley kept up his drive for public support by emphasizing the economic advantages to both the East and the West. By 1859 he had united two of his most important issues: federal aid for the transcontinental railroad and a free homestead. Some supporters of the railroad believed that a homestead law would make the land grants for railroad construction worthless. Greeley disagreed and countered that the offer of free land would attract so many immigrants to the West that the value of all property in the area, including the railroad land grants, would increase. As far as railroads east of the Mississippi, he had no doubt that they too would benefit from the movement of the "landless millions" from the East to homesteads in the West.[21]

In the spring of 1859 Greeley began an overland journey to the Pacific. His letters to the *Tribune* describing his adventures probably attracted more attention to the transcontinental railroad and the central route than any of his previous writings. He later wrote that he had resolved in 1848 to make the trip to study for himself the feasibility of building a railroad along the route. He wrote thirty-two articles along the way, beginning in Atchison, Kansas, and ending aboard the steamship *Golden* four months later.[22] The *Tribune* printed the articles as they arrived. He added a recap of his arguments for the railroad after he returned to New York. Later, Greeley gathered these letters for publication in *An Overland Journey from New York to San Francisco in the Summer of 1859.*[23]

Greeley wrote of his experiences but devoted most of the work to describing the wonders and opportunities of the western plains and California. He used the pages of the *Tribune* and *An Overland Journey* to encourage western settlement.

As he traveled across the West, people invited him to speak in nearly every town and settlement. He never refused, often telling his large audiences of the glories of the West, the advantages of a transcontinental railroad, and the virtues of the new Republican Party.

When he reached California in August 1859, he met with local Republican leaders. In Sacramento his advocacy of both his new party and the transcontinental railroad found an approving audience. Among Greeley's reception committee and hosts on a tour of the area were Collis Huntington, Mark Hopkins, and Charles Crocker. The fourth member of what would become the Central Pacific's "Big Four," Leland Stanford, was away campaigning as the Republican candidate for governor.[24] The editor's new acquaintances surely gave him plenty of ammunition for his fight for the railroad.

His last article about his trip, written in October 1859 after he returned to New York, asked and answered the question, Is there a national need of a railroad from the Missouri to the Pacific? He argued convincingly that between 1849 and 1857 381,107 people had traveled to California and 139,002 had returned. According to Greeley, nine-tenths of these people would have gone by train if one had been available, the fare moderate, and passage made in ten days. He believed that two or three times as many people would have traveled to California if a railroad had been available. Also, a railroad could carry at least $20 million in costly or perishable merchandise each year. The federal government, by Greeley's estimation, would add one million in revenue for transportation of mails and another three million for military men, munitions, and provisions. By adding passengers, freight, military provisions, and the mail, he calculated that a transcontinental railroad would earn at least $17 million annually.[25]

Fighting for the Railroad

The editor also evaluated the political and national ramifications of the railroad. He reasoned that not only would the federal government save money in moving the army to the West, but with improved transportation the nation could use its troops more efficiently and would, therefore, need fewer men in uniform. Even with a smaller army, the Pacific railroad and the telegraph would allow the country to defend both coasts against any attack. Such expediency would provide the United States more security at a lower cost.[26]

Greeley noted the "social, moral, and intellectual blessings of a Pacific railroad."[27] The delivery time for New York to California mail would decrease from thirty to ten days. Furthermore, California needed "a large influx" of women, and with the miserable six-thousand-mile journey by sea reduced to "a pleasant and interesting overland journey of ten days," at a lower cost, many more would make the trip. The railroad likewise would allow families with small children to migrate to California. The immigration of virtuous women and families would relieve the East of excess population and would bring willing workers and the "elements of moral and religious melioration" to California. Greeley's claims for the advantages of the Pacific railroad were almost without limits: "Civilization, intelligence, refinement, on both sides of the mountains . . . would receive a new and immense impulse, and the Union would acquire a greater accession of strength, power, endurance, and true glory, than it would from the acquisition of the whole continent down to the Cape Horn."[28]

After so decidedly "proving" the benefits of the railroad, the only points left for Greeley to consider were the practicality, cost, route, and financing of the venture. The army surveys a few years earlier had already verified that practicable routes existed, so he simply asserted that there was no doubt that the transcontinental railroad was realistic. Railroads in the East had encountered difficulties as great as any east of the Sierras. If the railroad simply followed the emigrant trail up the Platte River, then followed the Snake and Columbia on to Oregon, or through the South Pass to the foot of the Sierras, there would be no serious obstacles. Greeley also suggested a more central route along the Kansas and Arkansas Rivers, through the Rockies, across Utah to the Truckee River, then across the Sierra Nevadas to San Francisco.

Greeley admitted that the undertaking was too vast and too formidable for private financing. The task needed federal support. He called on Congress to approve the project, solicit bids, and provide $50 million in public aid to any responsible company that offered adequate security that it would complete construction within ten years. The builder should also receive land a mile wide on each side of the road and the right to take building materials from any public lands. In return the company had to agree to carry public mails at a reasonable rate, transport military troops and provisions at the lowest rates, and allow the federal government exclusive use of the line during national emergencies. He recommended that the lawmakers allow the construction company to choose the best route as long as it stayed entirely within U.S. territory. By following this plan, Greeley argued, the government could recoup its investment within five years from land sales, increased postage, and taxes on the increased sales of goods resulting from the presence of the railroad. Additionally, the nation would save millions of dollars in military transportation costs alone.[29]

The Pacific railroad, according to this ardent supporter, would contribute more to the nation's strength and wealth than "the acquisition of a dozen Cubas."[30] It would not only bind the nation closer together but also increase the national wealth. He proclaimed that the railroad would bring new vision to the nation and inspire its citizens toward wholesome achievements and away from filibustering. He concluded his article and *An Overland Journey* with the note that he had undertaken the trip to encourage the construction of the Pacific railroad and he hoped that his arduous journey had not been made in vain.[31]

Greeley's campaign for a railroad from the Mississippi or Missouri River to the Pacific Coast gained momentum in the months between his return to New York in October 1859 and the Republican National Convention in May 1860. He argued that the railroad was one of the country's most urgent needs and that it would earn more than $20 million the first year. He continued to call for federal support with terms similar to those in his October article. So when he traveled to Chicago for the convention, he brought his own agenda. He made his greatest contribution as a member of the party's platform committee, which included a plank resolving that the interests of the entire country demanded a Pacific railroad and that the federal government should aid in its construction. This resolution had greater impact than the similar one in 1856, because in 1860 it belonged to the party that won the election in November.[32]

But even after Abraham Lincoln's election, the railroad, like the homestead, took a back seat to more pressing matters. The withdrawal of southern opponents of the more northerly routes helped to unclog the logjam that had held up passage of a railroad bill. Although backers were confident that the enterprise would win federal support, they had to wait until the spring of 1862 before Congress found time to consider the matter. When Congress approved both a Homestead Act and a Pacific railroad bill on 6 May 1862, Greeley was ecstatic about the measures that provided free land for the landless and a transcontinental railroad to bind the country together. He exclaimed, "The clouds that have long darkened our National prospects are breaking away, and the sunshine of Peace, Prosperity and Progress will ere long irradiate the land. Let us rejoice in and gather strength from the Prospect."[33]

Two months later, on 1 July 1862, President Lincoln signed the bill into law. The measure chartered the Union Pacific Company to build the eastern part of a transcontinental railroad and the Central Pacific Company to build the western end. The federal government would grant the companies ten sections of public land for each mile of track and a loan of sixteen thousand dollars for each mile across the plains, thirty-two thousand for the foothills, and forty-eight thousand for the mountains. Even these seemingly generous terms did not attract investors, however. So in July 1864 Congress ceded to backers' exhortations and doubled the land grant and agreed to subordinate the federal loans to other mortgages the builders would need to secure sufficient money for the undertaking.[34]

Although these acts authorized the Central Pacific to build only to the California border, later amendments permitted the company to continue construction eastward until it met the Union Pacific line. The two roads met at Promontory Summit, Utah, on 10 May 1869, less than five years after construction began. A telegram to President Ulysses S. Grant announced the laying of the last rail and the driving of the last spike, 1,068 miles west of the Missouri River and 690 miles east of Sacramento.[35]

For two years after the completion of the railroad, Greeley continued to praise the blessings this achievement had brought to the country. Noting that the cost of transporting wheat had fallen from twenty cents per mile in 1850 to one and a quarter cents in 1870, he predicted that this "cheap and rapid trans-

Fighting for the Railroad

portation" would foster inestimable growth in American agriculture. This "first industry of mankind" had made fallow areas productive, created successful industries, and provided new experiences. To Greeley, the completion of the railroad across America was a peaceful conquest that compared favorably with any ever won by war. He eloquently concluded, "The stars in their courses are with us, and we bear the best hopes of Humanity."[36] Such were the gifts of the transcontinental railroad to agriculture and the nation.

But, Greeley claimed, agriculture was not the only industry to prosper because of the railroad; all American industry would benefit. He argued that the railroad doubled labor's efficiency and compensation by reducing the cost of moving products to the market.[37] Also, according to him, the prediction that the line would secure the trade with the Orient had proven to be true when the route across the United States completed the last link in a trade route that circled the globe. Although a change in trade patterns was not immediately apparent, he considered the expected economic boom in trade between the America and the Far East to be an "accomplished fact." He proclaimed that despite high railroad tariffs and traditional maritime traffic patterns, most of the American trade with the Orient and much of the European commerce was already moving over the new "permanent" route, which included the railroad across America.[38]

Greeley, not surprisingly, praised the railroad companies' efforts to populate the land acquired from the federal government. Unlike the earlier speculators whose acquisition of large tracts of land had thwarted the efforts of actual settlers, the companies "indorsed the American idea of Emigration" by providing easier passage for colonists, whether they were bound for railroad land or adjoining government property.

Greeley assured his readers that many people were responding to the railroads' call and moving West along their lines.

Greeley was so enamored with the Pacific railroad in 1870 and 1871 that he supported two more lines to the West Coast. Unlike his earlier preference for the northern route, in 1871 he said that the country especially needed the Southern Pacific Railroad. A railroad through Arizona would help protect the few settlers there. That territory, which he once deemed useless, now "teemed" with mineral wealth. So, he argued, the federal government should either build a railroad through the territory or withdraw the army and allow settlers to remain at their own peril.[39] When the Southern Pacific Railroad Bill came up for a vote in the Senate, he urged that body to approve the measure "without hesitation." After the Senate complied, Greeley had no doubt that President Grant would sign the bill. Later, when builders were considering a railroad across the northern plains to the Pacific, the editor supported it with equal fervor.[40]

Although the proposed Northern Pacific route from Minnesota to Puget Sound would open additional millions of acres of land on plains filled with lush vegetation, the railroad would have to induce immigrants to settle along the route before the line would be profitable. The Northern Pacific had an opportunity for "magnificent success" and a responsibility that Greeley described as almost a sacred trust: "It concerns not only the development of America, but the relief of Europe, and, in a great and incalculable measure, the civilization of the world." He then compared the builders to Moses and described the route itself as "a capacious and continuing city for all the wanderers of the earth."[41] Such was Greeley's eloquence and his poetic license when describing the railroads in 1871.

Disgust with the corruption of President Grant's adminis-

Fighting for the Railroad

tration forced Greeley to start separating himself from the party he had helped found. He opposed Grant's renomination until he realized it was futile to do so. Then, even though he was a member of the Republican National Committee, Greeley refused to attend its meetings or the national convention. He moved closer to the Liberal Republicans, a splinter group of reformers lead by Carl Schurz and Gratz Brown, who advocated tariff reform and universal amnesty and enfranchisement for former Confederate soldiers and government officials. Although Greeley supported amnesty and enfranchisement, especially for veterans of the Confederacy, the tariff reform smacked of "free trade" to him, and that he could not abide.[42]

The Liberal Republicans scheduled their convention for 1 May 1872 in Cincinnati, Ohio. Greeley, fearing that the delegates would include a plank for free trade in their platform, declined to attend, but sent his assistant editor, Whitelaw Reid, in his stead. Reid insisted that the committee exclude the tariff issue from the platform. Party leaders, realizing that this was the price for Greeley's support, agreed. The Liberal Republican convention, much to the chagrin of Schurz and other party leaders, then proceeded to nominate Greeley as the party candidate for president and Gratz Brown for vice president.[43]

Greeley's acceptance letter to the leaders of the convention, reproduced in the *Tribune* on 22 May 1872, reflected his change in attitude about the railroads. In this letter he "joyfully" adopted the "admirable" platform, citing specifically the resolution reserving public lands for cultivators instead of recklessly squandering them on the construction of railroads that no one needed and that plunged the country "into deeper and deeper abysses of foreign indebtedness."[44] Although Greeley had not helped write the platform, he openly embraced it. Still, throughout the campaign he seldom spoke of the platform issues, instead focusing his eloquence on the corruption in Washington and the virtue of limiting presidents to one term. Alas, although Greeley's readers loved and respected him, many preferred Grant as president. The champion of western causes received only 43.8 percent of the popular vote and carried only six states in the 1872 election. The following year the financial backing of the Northern Pacific Railroad collapsed and the Credit Mobilier scandal revealed the graft involved in building the Union Pacific line.

Horace Greeley's speeches, letters, books, and editorials had helped make a transcontinental railroad a reality. Greeley, the orator, spoke to thousands of people, on both his winter tours and his trip across the plains in 1859, about the advantages of a railroad line connecting western farmers to eastern cities and the excess of eastern workers to western land. Greeley, the politician, used his position as a party platform committee member to commit the Republicans to supporting a transcontinental railroad and used his position as a party leader to pressure congressmen into supporting the railroad in Congress. Greeley, the author, traveled across the plains and wrote of the blessings a railroad would bring to the West and the gifts that area would give to the rest of the country. Greeley, the editor, used the columns of the *Tribune* to tell his estimated one million readers that a railroad would increase the country's security, improve the prosperity of both the East and the West, and correct the maldistribution of population by moving workers from the overpopulated East to the underpopulated West. Greeley helped convince the American people and the American government to pay the enormous cost of building a railroad across the continent.

And what was that cost? From the time of the first federal support for the Illinois Central in 1850 until 1872, Congress

Fighting for the Railroad

granted about 130 million acres of public land to railroad builders, or about 9 percent of the public domain. Forty-five million of these acres went to the Union Pacific and the Central Pacific. The federal government also advanced about $64 million in government bonds, then had to spend decades in court trying to collect from the borrowers. The scandals of the 1870s revealed how much of the money went to pay for politicians' votes and to support the elegant life-styles of the builders.[45]

What had the American people bought? Greeley had led them to believe that the railroad would turn the West into the land of milk and honey. But western towns quickly learned otherwise: some died in the birthing when the railroads bypassed them; others found that the cost of bringing in the railroad bankrupted them and many of their leading citizens; nearly all quickly learned through excessive rates, rate discrimination, and favoritism toward communities where there was competition that the railroads were not benevolent companies. As one historian described it: "In popular fancy the railroads were transformed from gifts of a beneficent providence to dreadful vampires, the product of Satan, sucking the life blood of the country."[46]

Still, the railroads contributed more than any other institution to the opening of the West for settlement. The companies not only furnished the transportation but also provided the homestead. Then, to ensure that prospective settlers knew of the opportunity, railroad agents flooded the cities of the East and Europe, enticing people to the American West. Tens of thousands responded. Some became discouraged and moved on, others died from deprivation and disease; but enough survived and prospered that barely two decades later Turner could pronounce the area settled and the frontier gone.

6

SUPPORTING ASSOCIATION
AND THE UNION COLONY

Let our young men, or middle-aged men, or women if it must be, go out of the cities to push their fortunes, and go together. They will soon find out that, if two heads are better than one, so are two purses, and that hands and heads work best when they work in company and are willing to help each other.

Horace Greeley, 1 September 1871

A thousand heads of families, combining their means and efforts, may provide themselves with homes ... at half the cost, and with less than a tithe of the privation, involved in isolated pioneering.

Horace Greeley, 24 March 1870

In October 1869 Horace Greeley dispatched his agricultural editor, Nathan Meeker, to Utah to study and report on the Mormon community there. Greeley himself had visited Salt Lake City ten years earlier and had interviewed Brigham Young. Meeker rode the train west to the end of the Kansas Pacific line at Sheridan, Kansas, and then took a stage through Colorado on to Cheyenne, Wyoming. At Cheyenne, Greeley's emissary to the Mormons discovered that the snows had already come to the mountain passes and had closed the roads to Utah. While returning to New York by way of the Platte River Valley, Meeker conceived the idea for a "cooperative" colony in eastern Colorado. Although he wrote periodic letters, which Greeley published in the *Tribune*, Meeker did not mention his proposed undertaking until he returned to New York in late November 1869.[1]

After reaching home he first revealed his plan to his wife, Arvilla, who reluctantly consented to the pioneering venture. He then approached a "special friend," John Russell Young, the former managing editor of the *Tribune*. Young, who had visited Colorado, approved of the idea, and the two agreed that he would try to garner Greeley's support. Greeley was out of town at the time, so Young presented the proposal to him a few days later at a Press Club dinner at Delmonico's restaurant. The thought of a cooperative colony apparently reawakened Greeley's zeal for "Associationism" that had laid dormant for more than twenty years and rekindled the dream

Nathan Meeker, founder of the Union Colony.
(Courtesy City of Greeley Museums, Permanent Collection)

of the West as a safety valve. He sent the *Tribune*'s agricultural editor, J. B. Lyman, to find Meeker in the Delmonico crowd. Meeker confirmed his intention. Greeley expressed regrets that he could not accompany Meeker to Colorado but pledged his personal and editorial support and committed himself to the success of the colony.[2]

The mid-nineteenth century was a time of utopian experiments in America, many of which were along the western frontier.[3] Robert Dale Owen's New Harmony, Indiana, settlement in 1825 was an early attempt by an organized community to overcome the ills of industrialization. Greeley was well acquainted with Owen and his settlement. In 1860 the *Tribune* carried an ongoing debate between the two men on the place of marriage and divorce in American society. Greeley had also followed with interest the Mormon migration to Utah that began in 1847. In 1859 he visited Utah, interviewed Brigham Young, and observed the extensive irrigation system that allowed the Mormons to grow crops in the Great American Desert. Closer to home, Greeley belonged to the Brook Farm venture and eventually hired founder George Ripley and members Margaret Fuller and Charles A. Dana for the *Tribune*'s editorial staff.

Merging bits from these and other utopian socialist endeavors with the teachings of an obscure Frenchman, Greeley forged his solution for the "filth, squalor, rags, dissipation, want, and misery" that surrounded him in the winter of 1837–38. His series of articles in the *New Yorker* entitled "What shall be done for the Laborer?" caught the attention of Albert Brisbane. Brisbane had just returned from Paris, where he had studied Associationism under the tutelage of the movement's founder, Charles Fourier. In 1840 Brisbane published *The Social Destiny of Man*, detailing Fourier's teachings. Greeley read and admired the work, and the two met soon afterward.[4]

For a few weeks in 1841, Greeley published Brisbane's weekly newspaper, the *Future*. Beginning in March 1842 and continuing for more than a year, he printed Brisbane's columns on the new utopian socialism in the *Tribune*, then gathered the columns and published them in book form in 1843. Brisbane explained that an association was an assembly of four to eighteen hundred people who united to bring order and efficiency to their professions.[5] Fourier, according to Brisbane, believed there were 810 basic human types. Therefore, a group of sixteen to eighteen hundred people gathered into a "phalanx" would be large enough to produce a mixture of basic types and small enough to assure a close-knit community. The phalanx would live in a common building and work in collectively owned fields and industries. After ensuring a comfortable subsistence for everyone living in the phalanx, leaders would distribute the community's profits: seven-twelfths to laborers, three-twelfths to investors, and two-twelfths to contributors of "practical and theoretical Knowledge."[6]

Greeley especially approved Associationism's educational program, which chose the "fittest" people to be teachers and taught the children the educational fundamentals plus mechanics, chemistry, geology, botany, and the "love and practice of Industry." Under Associationism, Greeley believed, people would gladly and skillfully work; everyone, except the mentally or physically disabled, would earn enough to support themselves, and everyone could attain a "most thorough" education.[7] When his friend Rufus Griswold questioned whether people guaranteed food and shelter would be willing to work, Greeley expressed his belief that profits based on the hours, capital, and skills a person invested would inspire one to work for oneself at least as hard as one worked for wages.[8] Association seemed to offer a radical answer to urban poverty, but within a conservative framework. It would allow individuals to work in the careers for which they were best fitted, to receive training for their tasks, and to enjoy the "full reward" of their labors. Associationism, Greeley hoped, would achieve all this without forced revenue sharing or without disturbing private property rights.[9]

For the next five years, Greeley supported the movement not only in his paper but also in his practice. He attended conventions, organized phalanxes, belonged to three himself, served as treasurer of the Sylvania Phalanx in eastern Pennsylvania, and helped to convert the Brook Farm experiment to Associationism. In 1845 he pledged himself and his assets to the "common cause."[10]

During these years of avid support for Fourier's utopia, Greeley began to correspond with young Nathan Meeker, an officer of the Trumbull Phalanx at Braceville, Ohio. Even in the early 1840s Meeker had dreamed of a communal colony in the West.[11] After the Trumbull Phalanx failed, Meeker became a newspaper reporter. His writings caught Greeley's attention and, as the Civil War began, the editor told A. D. Richardson to hire Meeker as a war correspondent for the *Tribune.* After the war, Meeker moved to New York and joined the *Tribune* staff as agricultural editor.[12]

By the fall of 1846, Greeley's faith in Associationism as a safety valve had waned. A year earlier he had shifted to the radical idea that a free homestead would overcome urban workers' abject poverty. He would fight for a homestead law until it became a reality in 1862. He was not, however, ready to retract his words of praise for Associationism, especially in the face of criticism from his former protégé, *Courier and*

Supporting the Union Colony

Enquirer editor Henry J. Raymond. Between November 1846 and May 1847, the two traded barbs, criticisms, and insults in the columns of their respective papers. Although Greeley never admitted defeat, his support for association in the pages of the *Tribune* was never again as strong.[13] His dream of a utopian socialist community revived only after the Homestead Act of 1862 failed to be the panacea he had long predicted.

Years later he described Fourier as "erratic, mistaken, [and] visionary," but admitted borrowing from the Frenchman's teachings to create his own social creed.[14] In his autobiography, published in 1868, the year before Meeker's trip west, Greeley expressed his belief in "association," "cooperation," or any movement that united people to work toward a beneficent goal that was beyond a single person's capability.[15] He decried the "social anarchy" of what Americans would later call "rugged individualism" and praised the efficiency of production and consumption under association. He suggested that if four to five hundred families united and purchased two thousand acres, they could grow a variety of crops on less land with fewer draft animals. A group of this size could afford to build steam- or water-powered mills for sawing timber and grinding grain.[16] Attempts at such communal undertakings characterized the colony Meeker would found barely three years later. No wonder Greeley responded so positively when Meeker shared his dream in Delmonico's in November 1869.

Elated by Greeley's enthusiasm for the experiment, Meeker spent the next day writing an article for the *Tribune* announcing his intentions. After reviewing Meeker's plan, Greeley suggested dividing the proposed town into blocks of ten acres each. Meeker liked the idea and agreed to the change. Greeley then printed Meeker's letter on 4 December 1869, accompanied by his own editorial endorsing the venture. Greeley praised the eastern Colorado location for its healthful climate, fertility, ease of cultivation, abundance of timber, and plentiful supply of water for irrigation, adding that when the railroad was complete, travelers could reach the area within three days from St. Louis or five from New York. He praised Meeker as a "practical" farmer, who was "eminently" qualified to found and lead the colony. The editor then advised "temperate, moral, industrious, intelligent" men, with an interest in moving to the West, to read Meeker's letter.[17]

In his open letter, Meeker explained his plan to unite with "proper" people to establish a colony in Colorado Territory and invited temperate men of means to join him. He described the area's rich soil, "healthful" climate, groves of pine trees, and abundant supply of water. Although he promised that colonists could obtain 160 acres of this Eden for eighteen dollars, this estimate proved to be overly optimistic. Recalling his experience with the poorly financed Trumbull Phalanx, Meeker insisted that the colonists include at least fifty settlers. Of the settlers, there should be either ten people with ten thousand dollars each or twenty people with five thousand dollars each. The remainder needed at least two hundred to one thousand dollars.[18] By directing his appeal to people of means, Meeker did much to ensure the project's survival. Greeley later reconciled the apparent disparity between this plan, which catered to the more affluent settlers, and his vision of the West as a safety valve for the urban East's poor. He acknowledged that not everyone could pay their own way to Colorado, but explained that every person who moved West would leave a space for someone lower on the "ladder" to "ascend a round or two."[19]

Meeker envisioned families living in a village and tilling a 40-to-160-acre plot nearby. He would sell the town lots at an auction to raise money for a church, a town hall, a schoolhouse, and a library. Such public buildings would increase the value of the town lots "five to ten times," he believed. By settling in a community, the colonists would have immediate access to public facilities and other benefits of society. He called for the professionals and skilled workers to join him in forming "an intelligent, educated and thrifty community," a community that would proudly exhibit modern civilization's best traits. He invited qualified people interested in the enterprise to write him at the *Tribune*'s office and asked them to enclose their occupation and an estimate of the value of the property they would take to Colorado.[20]

On 17 December the *Tribune* announced a meeting on the twenty-third at Cooper Institute so perspective emigrants could learn more about the venture. At one o'clock that Thursday afternoon, Horace Greeley, the meeting's appointed chairman, first shared his vision of a thousand colonies, similar to the one Meeker proposed, spreading across the West. Having advocated western migration as the answer to eastern urban poverty for nearly thirty years, the editor admitted, "I do not know whether emigration is the best remedy, but I think so."[21] He then introduced Meeker to the overflowing crowd.

Meeker announced that more than eight hundred people with an estimated personal worth of more than $1 million had already written asking to accompany him to Colorado. The group represented all trades and professions, he said, but most were farmers. He proceeded to describe the proposed settlement to the crowd. Although Meeker revealed that he had not yet selected the exact spot for the colony, he listed what he considered the most important characteristics for the site: a healthful climate, soil rich enough for grass to grow naturally and fruit trees to thrive, coal or timber for fuel, a supply of iron ore, and enough water to irrigate the crops and provide a power supply for the mills. Together the colonists would build schools, churches, and the other amenities necessary for a "civilized community"; Meeker, therefore, informed the "idle, immoral, intemperate, [and] inefficient" that they need not apply.[22]

When discussing the possible difficulties of the venture, Meeker admitted that crops would not grow in eastern Colorado without the benefit of irrigation. Greeley later returned to the podium and affirmed his belief in irrigation. Coincidentally, he had traveled through the area where Meeker proposed to settle in 1859 and had described the soil and topography as inferior, but similar to that of Lombardy, and predicted that like that famous region in northern Italy, eastern Colorado would thrive when farmers introduced "systematic" irrigation. Now, ten years later, he emphasized that a small amount of water, properly applied, could produce surprising results. He asserted, as an example, that even in water-starved California, farmers used much more water than was necessary to grow their crops.[23] Both Meeker and Greeley were right! Crops grew well in eastern Colorado, but only with the benefit of irrigation.

The prospective emigrants voted to call their new home the Union Colony and elected Meeker president and Greeley treasurer of the Union Colony Association.[24] Fifty-nine members immediately paid five dollars for initial expenses; others promised to mail payment to Greeley at the *Tribune*. All members committed themselves to paying $150, by 15 February 1870, to purchase land in eastern Colorado. Meeker recommended that the members appoint a committee to find the best location for the colony.[25]

The locating committee, comprised of Meeker, colony vice president "General" R. A. Cameron, and Henry T. West, took the Union Pacific Railroad west about six weeks later, in February 1870, in search of the right spot. By this time the rail system extended into Colorado, so they switched to the Denver Pacific and rode it to the terminus at Evans. Before the committee had left New York, Greeley advised Meeker to seek a place where sugar beets could be an "*ultimate*" crop. One where corn, peaches, and grapes would grow.[26] Meeker apparently mentioned to Greeley the possibility of looking for land in Utah. The editor wrote to Meeker shortly after the locating committee headed west discouraging him from going to Salt Lake and questioning whether Utah could provide as much water for both irrigation and power as the area in Colorado where the Boulder, Thompson, and Horse Creeks flowed from the mountains.[27]

Meeker had intended to locate near Pike's Peak, but that site was too small for an agricultural colony. Another plot near Pueblo was not conducive to the construction of irrigation canals. Eventually, after investigating other possibilities, the committee selected the spot where the Cache la Poudre River flows into the Platte, a few miles north of where Thompson Creek joined the same river at Evans and very near the location Greeley had recommended in his letter.[28] The 6 April 1970 *Tribune* carried Meeker's telegram announcing the location of Union Colony Number One.[29]

In a later edition, Meeker wrote of the rich soil, beautiful scenery, and the trout-filled river that would provide an ample supply of water for irrigation. When the Rocky Mountain snows melted in June and July, settlers could float timber down the Cache la Poudre from the nearby forests. He also described the abundant grass that would feed the livestock.[30] The committee had not found free land, but had paid previous settlers and the Denver Pacific Railroad Company sixty thousand dollars for twelve thousand acres along the river. Meeker and the others also committed the association to buying another fifty thousand acres within three years from the Denver Pacific for between three and four dollars an acre, depending upon the date of actual purchase.[31]

After locating the site for their new community, Meeker, Cameron, and West drew up a charter for the Union Colony of Colorado. Although both Cameron and West wanted to name the town Meeker for the association's president, he would have none of it. They finally agreed to call it Greeley, in honor of their supporter and benefactor.[32] Meeker's son Ralph would later explain that his father was grateful to Greeley for accepting the role of treasurer and adding his name to the endeavor: Meeker and the committee realized that Greeley was well known and had a reputation for honesty and fairness.[33] Back in New York, Greeley, too, had been busy. As treasurer, he collected the $150 membership fee from the Union Colony association's 442 members. He informed Meeker on 19 February 1870 that the treasury had already climbed to nearly thirty thousand dollars,[34] including one thousand dollars of his own money.[35] By the time of Meeker's announcement on 6 April, the colony's reserves had apparently grown to nearly sixty thousand dollars as four hundred members had paid in full.[36]

Greeley also used the pages of his paper to renew his call for emigration to the West. He proclaimed that hundreds of thousands of poor people with little more than the clothes they wore had emigrated to the West and had built "bounteous farms and pleasant homes."[37] He later discouraged settlers from setting out alone, but recommended "Concerted Emigration," similar to the organized colonization taking place in the Union Colony (although he did not mention the colony by name). "Plunging *alone* into the wilderness," he warned, was "a rugged enterprise" that often required, because of the primitive conditions, twenty years to build a farm. The lack of

Supporting the Union Colony

roads and the long distances to needed services created great obstacles for the settlers. Concerted emigration, however, would eliminate or at least ameliorate these problems. A thousand families working together could provide themselves with homes at half the cost and at a tenth of the deprivation of each family moving and working alone. Again the editor encouraged the people of New York to move west, claiming that fifty thousand families living in the city should immediately join in a concerted emigration.[38]

Greeley, however, aimed most of his energy and advice directly at the colony. He planned to emphasize his support by speaking at the town's first Independence Day celebration in 1870. Ill health, however, forced him to delay his visit until 12 October. Denver's *Daily Rocky Mountain News* recorded the event, describing his enthusiastic welcome by a large crowd that broke into three cheers as he alit from the train. The crowd escorted the celebrated editor up the street to the *Greeley Tribune,* a weekly whose first edition Meeker would release a few days later. From a hastily constructed stand in front of the newspaper building, Greeley applauded the colony's excellent locality and spoke of the advantages of having a railroad so near. Turning to practical matters, he suggested that farmers "herd" their livestock, instead of incurring the expense of building fences. Then, returning to one of his favorite subjects, he urged them to build irrigation canals rather than depend on the vagaries of the weather to water their crops. He related his own observations from travel in Europe and reminded the crowd that early agriculture in the Nile Valley had depended on irrigation.[39] David Boyd, who wrote an eyewitness account of the settlement of the colony, recalled that Greeley spoke to the "people in a calm, fatherly way, giving them what he believed [to be] good, practical advice."[40]

First settlers in Greeley, Colorado, in 1870.
(Courtesy City of Greeley Museums, Permanent Collection)

A reporter for the *Daily Colorado Tribune,* writing of Greeley's visit, described the town of Greeley, with an estimated population of eight hundred people. Thousands of "soft" maple trees lined the wide streets. The young community boasted of twelve to fifteen stores, including two jewelry stores, two blacksmith shops, and two drug stores. The prohibition against the sale of alcohol, except at the drug stores for medicinal purposes, perhaps explains how only eight hundred people could support two such pharmacies in the same town. A "book, periodical, and stationery" store catered to the reading and writing public. Greeley also had a hotel, which the reporter assured his readers was "as good as circumstance [would] allow." Summarizing his impression of the townspeople, the reporter remarked, "Sobriety, good order, peace, harmony and prosperity, characterize the people of this colony."[41] The sobriety, good order, and ban on alcohol earned the community the epithet "Angels' Roost." The man for whom the town was named told another reporter he expected the town to prosper, unless the citizens began drinking, gambling, or "some kindred folly." This he did not expect.[42]

Supporting the Union Colony

Greeley maintained close contact with Meeker and Union Colony, sharing his advice on how to make the enterprise prosper. Meeker listened and tried to heed his old friend's recommendations. Greeley warned the colony against concentrating on cash crops before it had supplied its own food, and suggested that colonists spend the first five years erecting farm buildings and fences, preparing their soil, and digging canals to bring the precious water to their crops.[43] Concerned that the settlers would concentrate on creating a town and neglect the farming, he encouraged Meeker to strive to plant fifteen thousand acres in crops by the end of 1871. To Greeley, farm production was second only to shelter in importance for the colony's survival. But he feared that more people would be selling "tape and candy" than would be spending their days plowing the land.[44]

Greeley's suggestions were not all gems. Although he was well versed in the agricultural wisdom of his day, he like many other "experts" tried to apply eastern experience to western conditions. He constantly advised Meeker on how to tend the plot of two and a half acres that Greeley had received from the colony as a token payment for his services. The big city editor who aspired to be a farmer determined trees to be the ideal crop for his acreage in this treeless plain, without considering why the plain might be treeless. His insistence on raising trees on the property and Meeker's persistent attempts to comply with Greeley's wishes were almost humorous. Greeley first asked Meeker to plant locust seeds, adding that he hoped to be able to add hickory nuts, white oak acorns, and white pine seeds later.[45] Meeker planted one thousand small evergreens and two thousand larches in the spring and, with great difficulty, kept them watered. A few lived until the following year, then they, too, died.[46] Greeley continued to dream of trees so thick on his lot that they required thinning. Such abundant growth, he told Meeker, would control the weeds.[47] He admitted that planting the evergreens had been a mistake and instructed Meeker to plant acorns, hickory nuts, and chestnuts.[48] Meeker complied. Only a few plants came up, and most of those soon died. The magnificent oaks Greeley envisioned grew to only a few inches before they died. Still he persisted. Meeker next planted black walnuts, but the harsh winter killed them all.[49] Despite overwhelming evidence to the contrary, Greeley clung to his belief that eastern trees would grow on the western plains. In one of his last letters to Meeker, he instructed his friend not to "starve" his trees and to consider planting more on an adjacent lot.[50]

Financial support and solid fiscal advice were Greeley's other contributions to the colony. Besides his initial membership fee, he invested additional thousands of dollars in land in the colony and periodically lent Meeker money, including one thousand dollars in 1870.[51] Greeley made both the investments and the loans to help the colony overcome financial crises. He even bought back shares from disgruntled colonists, including Miss Mary L. Price of Planesville, Pennsylvania, because he believed dissatisfied investors would be detrimental to the group.[52] He advised Meeker to do the same to stop the noise of the grumblers, who were harming the colony. In another letter he expressed the desire to "stop the grumblers' mouths," because they were people who could only help the colony by leaving it.[53]

When the colony undertook the large task of building the canals needed to irrigate the crops, a debate arose over whether to finance the project by borrowing the money or by selling land. Greeley was adamant against borrowing and expressed his "horror of debt." He proposed, instead, that the

Supporting the Union Colony

leaders sell communal lands to raise the money. They could buy the land back when the need arose.[54] He doubted, in fact, that the colony could borrow enough to complete the project. Even if it could, he did not think it wise. He told Meeker that indebtedness was a "poison" that always proved fatal for a cooperative.[55]

The people of Union Colony heeded Greeley's admonition. They sold community property to raise cash and did much of the canal building themselves. The editor congratulated Meeker on the decision to "dig out, rather than to borrow out. Borrowing out is only getting deeper in."[56] Union Colony historian David Boyd later recalled Greeley's counsel and acknowledged that other settlements in the area borrowed to build their canals and then failed when they could not pay the mortgages. Boyd believed that Greeley's advice and assistance helped the colony to survive a crucial period in its early existence.[57]

Horace Greeley's contributions to the settlement of the Union Colony and the founding of Greeley, Colorado, were both direct and indirect. By winning the editor's support and adding his name to the undertaking, first by having him serve as treasurer, then by giving the town his name, Meeker wrapped this idealistic project with a cloak of honesty, integrity, and legitimacy. Union Colony immediately benefited from the reputation that Greeley had built after many years as editor of the nation's most powerful newspaper. Greeley as treasurer also explains much of the success of collecting the membership fees to purchase the land.

Although Greeley invested substantially in the colony, the value of his counsel was probably second only to his good name. Having visited eastern Colorado himself, he supported a colony there. By coincidence or design, Meeker settled near the area that Greeley had recommended. Long an advocate of

Detail of an artist's rendering of Greeley, Colorado, in 1882.
(Courtesy City of Greeley Museums, Permanent Collection)

irrigation, he realized the necessity of building a system to bring water to the crops. David Boyd believed Greeley helped the colony avoid the pitfalls of credit, which allowed it to survive while similar attempts failed because of heavy debt. He used the columns of the *Tribune,* personal letters to Meeker, and a speech in the town of Greeley to express his ideas to the colony's leaders and people. Ralph Meeker later acknowledged the colony's obligation to Greeley for its survival.

Delores Hayden, in a recent work on utopian communities, described the contemporary community of Greeley, Colorado, as an agricultural center with a university and about forty thousand people (1990 population was about sixty thousand).

Supporting the Union Colony

But she considered the town a failure as a utopian experiment because the colonists abandoned most of their communal institutions within four years of the colony's birth. According to Hayden, the resultant town was "indistinguishable" from many others in the area.[58]

True, the Union Colony did not follow the path of other utopian communities. It had neither the rigid structure of New Harmony nor the idealism of Brook Farm. It also failed to maintain the cohesion that helped the Mormons thrive in Utah. But despite Greeley's lofty dreams of a thousand similar colonies in the West, Union Colonists had more limited goals. Apparently, most were people with at least limited assets who wanted to improve their lives. Together they proved the value of what Greeley called "concerted emigration." Within a matter of months the settlers had recreated a microcosm of their eastern society—with stores, a newspaper, and a hotel—and had begun an extensive irrigation system. Western historian Rodman Paul credited the "Greeley Colony" with developing much of the knowledge of irrigation that is still used in the West today, although that credit probably belongs to the Mormons.[59] Another trait that distinguished Greeley from other towns in the region was that it was a "planned settlement" created by and for families, not a "boom town" that grew up around a gold strike. When people moved to Greeley, they planned to stay. This set Greeley apart and helped the town survive. Perhaps as a utopian community, the Union Colony failed. But as an example of people banding together, pooling their resources, and creating a home for themselves and their families, the colony succeeded. Greeley deserves some credit for that success.

EPILOGUE

He was not only unlike other men—he was unlike himself often.

Tribune *employee Junius Browne*

In May 1872, with his nomination for president, Horace Greeley reached the pinnacle of his political career. Although he had repeatedly disavowed any desire for political favor or reward, he constantly lamented that he did not receive enough recognition from his party for his contributions. His nomination as the candidate of first the Liberal Republicans and then the Democrats finally brought him the acclaim he believed he deserved. On 22 May he printed his letter of acceptance in the *Tribune*.

A week earlier the paper had carried another personal notice from its editor. He acknowledged that his "unexpected" nomination had presented him with the dilemma of trying to be both journalist and candidate. Because he did not believe he could successfully do both, Greeley announced his withdrawal as editor of the *Tribune*, stating that until further notice he would exercise no control over the paper.[1]

Throughout the summer and early autumn of 1872, Greeley, in a departure from the presidential candidates' usual practices, hit the campaign trail. He traveled from the Northeast to the Midwest, promising to clean up the corruption that had followed Grant to Washington. He conveniently avoided mentioning the divergent platforms of the two parties he represented. In early October, results from states with early election days presaged Grant's landslide victory. Republican voters were unwilling to abandon the party and the man who had won the Civil War; and Democrats were less than enthusiastic

Epilogue

about the man who had insulted them in his paper for the past thirty years. Greeley carried only six states and received less than 44 percent of the total vote.

As devastating as this humiliating defeat must have been for Greeley, two other losses that occurred at the same time were even greater. On 30 October, a week before the general election confirmed the magnitude of his political defeat, his wife Molly died. Although he had often neglected her for politics and the *Tribune,* her loss drove him deeper into despair. He wrote a friend, "I am not dead but wish I were. My house is desolate, my future dark, my heart a stone."[2]

After burying Molly, Greeley announced in the *Tribune* on 7 November that he was resuming his position as editor. The decision did not please many on the paper's staff. One writer inserted an editorial comment that derided Greeley as a defeated candidate without influence. When the old editor demanded that the paper print a retraction, his protégé Whitelaw Reid, the managing editor, refused, fearing the editorial staff would walk out en masse. With that, Greeley learned that he no longer controlled the paper he had founded and nurtured to greatness. After losing his wife, his dream of being president, and control of his beloved *Tribune,* a scant three weeks later, on 29 November 1872, Greeley died.

If Greeley spent any of his final days reflecting on his life and his attempt to solve the dilemma of the urban poor, it would be interesting to know how he evaluated his efforts. Horace Greeley was a brilliant thinker, a capable writer, and a great editor. His vision for America, however, was based more on borrowed ideas than original thoughts. Thomas Jefferson and others before him praised the virtues of the farmer and the agrarian society. Thomas Carlyle claimed that governments could eliminate social injustice by providing land to the poor and encouraging their migration from the cities. George Henry Evans and the National Reformers began the cry for free land in the West for America's poor. Robert Mills, Hartwell Carter, Asa Whitney, and an unnamed host of others were on the transcontinental railroad bandwagon long before Greeley took up the cause. Robert Dale Owen established New Harmony in 1825, when Greeley was a mere boy of fourteen. Even "Go West! young man!" apparently originated with John Soule, not Horace Greeley.

Greeley's gift lay not in original thinking but in assimilating the divergent ideas of others, devising a creative solution to a major social problem, then devoting his considerable talent and influence to make the vision a reality. Believing that farming was a noble profession and assuming that with adequate knowledge almost anyone could succeed at it, he set about to educate his readers. America's farmers benefitted from Greeley's efforts. Columns in the Tribune on fertilizers, soil enhancers, crop rotation, irrigation, improved methods, new equipment, and other innovations increased production. Furthermore, the land-grant colleges he helped create have taught tens of thousands of farmers how to grow more and better crops. The Department of Agriculture, another of his visions, introduced American farmers to new products and methods from around the world and developed worldwide markets for American agricultural products.

As he worked to turn city dwellers into farmers and to educate them in their new profession, he tried to provide them with land. The Panic of 1837 converted New York City from a city of prosperity to a city of despair and converted Greeley from a conservative to a radical on land reform. The Homestead Act, which finally became law in 1862 and which Greeley promoted as a panacea for the urban poor, had little effect on them. They were not the ones who took advantage of the act, and the farmers who did needed more than free land to be successful. They had to have money for seed, equipment, livestock, and food and shelter until their first harvest. Also, the law did not protect against speculation and it did not work in the semiarid area west of the one hundredth meridian. Yet by the end of the nineteenth century, hundreds of thousands of homesteaders had claimed more than seventy million acres on the Great Plains.

Greeley knew that free land would be of little use to independent farmers if they had to compete with slave labor. So while he strived to make land available, he did everything he could to prevent slave owners from extending their "peculiar institution" into these new lands. In the struggle to keep slavery from spreading to the western territories, Greeley lost several battles but helped win the war. He and the Republican Party played an important part in keeping slavery out of Kansas and the West; but their stand against the extension of slavery added fuel to the fire that soon led to the great civil war that enveloped and threatened the entire nation.

Greeley's vision of the West also included a transcontinental railroad, which would ease the passage of immigrants to the West, transport their produce to eastern markets, and bind the nation together. As with the Homestead Act, not all the effects of the transcontinental railroad were positive. Instead of a line that blessed everyone along its path, as Greeley had predicted, the railroads blessed some and damned others. The builders often grew rich, whereas investors seldom recouped their money. Some towns boomed because of the railroads, others busted. Exorbitant or discriminatory rates favored large shippers and penalized the small western farmers Greeley promised to help. Still, the railroads carried people

to the land and farm products to market and recruited settlers from across the United States and Europe to occupy the
millions of acres along the rail lines. The transcontinental railroad made the country a more cohesive unit by cutting the
travel time from Atlantic to Pacific from weeks to days. Railroads eventually contributed more than any other institution
to the opening of the West for settlement.

Although many of Greeley's plans for settlement were practical, his favorite method was visionary. Believing that the
mutual support offered through the utopian socialist principles
of association would enhance western farmers' chances of survival, Greeley advocated group or colonial settlement. When
Nathan Meeker tried a modified association settlement at
Union Colony, Colorado, Greeley supported him with his paper, his advice, and his money. His vision of a thousand similar settlements never came to be, but the survival and growth
of Union Colony testifies that even Greeley's most radical
ideas had some merit.

Consider again the rhetorical question: In November 1872,
how would Greeley have assessed his efforts to people the West
with New York City's poor? Surely he must have seen that the
West was filling up, but in 1872 there were more poor in New
York than when he began his work thirty-five years earlier.
This reformer's compassion was counterbalanced by an ego
that prevented him from seeing many of his mistakes and from
admitting the ones that others pointed out. He probably could
have saved face by claiming either that many poor New York-
ers did move but European immigrants took their place or
that speculators, corrupt politicians, and railroad men
thwarted his efforts.

"Alas!" one could cry, "Greeley devoted his life to a lost
cause." It is true that Greeley did not understand the dynam-

ics of the westward expansion in the mid-nineteenth century. Still, he was an important participant in the process. In 1820 barely one-quarter of the U.S. population lived west of the Appalachian Mountains; forty years later, about half the nation's 31.4 million people lived there. New York City's poor might not have heard Greeley's call to go west, but millions of others did. And the Homestead Act, the absence of slavery, the information on the latest developments in agriculture, and the transcontinental railroad helped make their migration and settlement much easier. His were not wasted efforts, although he misjudged who the beneficiaries would be. Twenty-one years after Greeley's death, Frederick Jackson Turner wrote his paper, "The Significance of the Frontier in American History." Based on many of the same assumptions as Greeley's plan to alleviate poverty, it was a fitting conclusion to Greeley's call, "Go West, young man!"

NOTES

PREFACE

1. John B. L. Soule, of the Terre Haute, Indiana, *Express,* apparently originated the phrase "Go West, Young Man!" Greeley, however, was the person who popularized it.
2. James Parton, *The Life of Horace Greeley, Editor of the New York Tribune* (Boston: Fields & Osgood, 1869).
3. Henry Nash Smith, *Virgin Land: The American West as Symbol and Myth* (New York: Alfred A. Knopf, 1950), 234.

INTRODUCTION: GREELEY AND THE SAFETY VALVE

1. Frederick Jackson Turner, "Contributions of the West to American Democracy," *The Frontier in American History,* 259. This first appeared in the *Atlantic Monthly,* January 1903.
2. Horace Greeley, *Recollections of a Busy Life* (New York: J. B. Ford, 1868), 95.
3. Ibid., 145.
4. Robert H. Bremner, *From the Depths: The Discovery of Poverty in the United States* (New York: New York University Press, 1956), 3, 17–18.
5. Greeley, *Recollections,* 145.
6. Raymond Williams, *The Country and the City* (London:

Chatto & Windmus, 1973) traces this theme back to the beginning of English history.

7. Morton and Lucia White, *The Intellectual Versus the City* (Cambridge: Joint Center for Urban Studies, 1962), 27, 31.

8. Ray Allen Billington, *America's Frontier Heritage* (San Francisco: Holt, Rinehart and Winston, 1966), 30.

9. Bremner, *From the Depths*, 35–38.

10. Ibid., 38–41.

11. *New York Tribune*, 18 April 1856.

12. Ibid., 17 December 1842; 19 July, 31 July 1843.

13. Ibid., 20 July 1847, 1 April 1858.

14. Horace Greeley, *An Overland Journey: From New York to San Francisco in the Summer of 1859*, ed. Charles T. Duncan (New York: Alfred A. Knopf, 1964), 7.

15. *New York Tribune*, 23 February 1854, 7 December 1844.

16. Ibid., 1 April 1858.

17. Ibid., 2 February 1843.

18. Ibid.

19. Ibid., 11 June 1845.

20. Greeley, *Recollections*, 360.

21. *New York Tribune*, 11 June 1847, 8 March 1850.

22. Greeley, *Recollections*, 384.

23. Ibid.

24. *New York Tribune*, 24 March 1870.

25. Ibid., 18 July 1842.

26. Ibid., 21 July 1843.

CHAPTER 1: EDITOR AND ADVOCATE OF THE WEST

1. Horace Greeley to Moses Cortland, 14 April 1845, Greeley Collection, New York Public Library (hereafter cited as Greeley Collection–New York). This letter contains much autobiographical information on Greeley.

2. Greeley, *Recollections*, 84.

3. Ibid., 92–93.

4. Greeley later incorporated this magazine into the *Weekly Tribune* in 1841. It had no connection to the modern magazine of the same name.

5. Greeley, *Recollections*, 95.

6. Ibid., 126.

7. Ibid., 134.

8. Ibid., 136.

9. Richard Kluger, *The Paper: The Life and Death of the New York Herald Tribune* (New York: Alfred A. Knopf, 1986), 14.
10. Greeley, *Recollections,* 139, 140.
11. Ibid., 138.
12. Greeley to Griswold, 4 August 1841, Greeley Collection, Huntington Library, San Marino, California. (hereafter cited as Greeley Collection–Huntington).
13. Glyndon G. Van Deusen, *Horace Greeley: Nineteenth-Century Crusader* (Philadelphia: University of Pennsylvania Press, 1953), 57.
14. Ibid., 81.
15. Allan Nevins, *American Press Opinion* (New York: D. C. Heath, 1928), 112–13.
16. Greeley, *Recollections,* 119.
17. *New York Tribune,* 2 February, 19 July, 25 November 1843.
18. Van Deusen, *Horace Greeley,* 92.
19. Ibid., 112.
20. Greeley, *Recollections,* 292–93.
21. Ibid., 217.
22. Van Deusen, *Horace Greeley,* 127.
23. Greeley to Griswold, 21 January 1849, Greeley Collection, Boston Public Library (hereafter cited as Greeley Collection–Boston).
24. Greeley, *Recollections,* 233.
25. Nativists, who were an anti-Catholic and antiforeigner, banded together into secret Order of the Star Spangled Banner societies and became a strong political force in the 1850s as the American party. Because of their refusal to reveal information about the societies, members became popularly known as the Know-Nothings.
26. Van Deusen, *Horace Greeley,* 184–92.
27. Wilkeson to Seward, 1 June 1858, Seward Collection, University of Rochester.
28. Horace Greeley, *A History of the Struggle for Slavery Extension or Restriction in the United States, from the Declaration of Independence to the Present Day. Mainly compiled and condensed from the journals of the Congress and other official records, and showing the vote by yeas and nays on the important divisions in either house* (New York: Dix, Edwards, 1856).
29. Kluger, *The Paper,* 92.

30. Herndon to Greeley, 8 April 1858, Greeley Collection–New York.
31. Herndon to Greeley, 20 July 1858, Greeley Collection–New York.
32. Greeley, *Recollections,* 358.
33. Robert L. Perkin, *The First Hundred Years: An Informal History of Denver and the Rocky Mountain News* (New York: Doubleday, 1959), 97–119.
34. William Harlan Hale, *Horace Greeley, Voice of the People* (New York: Harper and Brothers, 1950), 226. Kluger and others corroborated these figures.
35. Kluger, *The Paper,* 14.
36. Horace Greeley and John F. Cleveland, *A Political Textbook for 1860: Comprising a Brief View of Presidential Nominations and Elections including All the National Platforms ever yet Adopted: also, A History of the Struggle respecting Slavery in the Territories, and of the action of Congress as to the Freedom of the Public Lands, with the most notable speeches and letters of Messrs. Lincoln, Douglas, Bell, Cass, Seward, Everett, Breckenridge, H.V. Johnson, etc., etc., touching the question of the day; and returns of all presidential elections since 1836* (New York: Tribune Association, 1860).
37. Van Deusen, *Horace Greeley,* 247. The Blairs were a powerful political family. Francis Blair ran the *Washington Globe* and had supported Andrew Jackson. He was also active in the founding of the Republican party. Montgomery, one of Frank Blair's sons, became Lincoln's first postmaster general.
38. Charles A. Dana, *Recollections of the Civil War* (New York: D. Appleton, 1913), 171.
39. Seward to Greeley, 3 December 1867, Greeley Collection, Library of Congress.
40. Greeley to Mrs. R. M. Whipple, 7 December 1867, Greeley Collection–Huntington.
41. George Bidwell to Greeley, 13 March 1869, Greeley Collection–New York.
42. Greeley to Colfax, 7 November 1870, Greeley Collection–New York.

Chapter 2: Educating Farmers for Their Noble Profession

1. Kluger, *The Paper,* 51.
2. Ibid., 50, 92.

3. Paul W. Gates, *The Farmer's Age: Agriculture 1815–1860* (New York: Holt, Rinehart and Winston, 1960), 340.
4. Greeley, *Recollections*, 295.
5. Greeley, *What I Know of Farming*, 184.
6. *New York Tribune*, 15 July 1842.
7. Ibid., 31 December 1843, 18 April 1858.
8. Ibid., 21 December 1848, 4 July 1857, 18 April 1858.
9. Greeley, *Overland Journey*, 302.
10. *New York Tribune*, 6 May 1852, 5 February 1859.
11. Greeley, *What I Know of Farming*, 17, 25.
12. *New York Tribune*, 16 November 1869.
13. Greeley, *Recollections*, 296.
14. Greeley, *What I Know of Farming*, 199.
15. Ibid., 197.
16. Van Deusen, *Horace Greeley*, 146.
17. Greeley, *Recollections*, 297–300.
18. See chapter 6, on the settlement of Union Colony, for more details.
19. Greeley, *Recollections*, 306–9.
20. Ibid., 310.
21. *New York Tribune*, 2 May 1843.
22. *New York Tribune*, 31 December 1843; 8 October 1852; 3 July, 12 October, 27 November 1855.
23. Greeley, *What I Know of Farming*, 25.
24. Ibid., 85–90.
25. Ibid., 92.
26. Ibid., 92–98.
27. Ibid., 108.
28. Ibid., 120.
29. Ibid., 79.
30. Ibid., 82.
31. Ibid., 84.
32. Ibid., 129–32.
33. Greeley, *Recollections*, 298.
34. Ibid., 304.
35. Greeley, *What I Know of Farming*, 55.
36. Ibid., 46.
37. Ibid.
38. Ibid., 299–301.
39. Ibid., 239–40.
40. Ibid., 94.

41. Ibid:, 243–44.
42. *Tribune,* 2 May 1852.
43. Ibid.
44. Greeley, *What I Know of Farming,* 196.
45. *New York Tribune,* 26 June 1851.
46. Ibid., 14 February 1844.
47. Ibid., 8, 28 February 1859.
48. Ibid., 8 February 1859.
49. Ibid., 21 June 1862.
50. Allan Nevins, *The Origins of the Land-Grant Colleges and State Universities* (Washington D. C.: Civil War Centennial Commission, 1962), 3, 7.
51. *New York Tribune,* 21 June 1862.
52. Ibid.

CHAPTER 3: ADVOCATING LAND REFORM AND THE HOMESTEAD ACT

1. *New Yorker,* 15 October 1836, 18 February 1837.
2. Van Deusen, *Horace Greeley,* 28–32.
3. *New Yorker,* 23 September and 7 October 1837; *Jeffersonian,* 16 and 23 June 1838.
4. Greeley, *Recollections,* 145.
5. *New Yorker,* 22 April 1837.
6. Greeley, *Recollections,* 310.
7. *New Yorker,* 3 June 1837.
8. *New York Tribune,* 18 April 1858.
9. *New Yorker,* 17 June 1837.
10. *New York Tribune,* 15 June 1843.
11. Ibid., 28 May 1841.
12. *New Yorker,* 3 February, 25 August 1838; *Jeffersonian,* 23 June, 8 September 1838; *Log Cabin,* 4 September 1841.
13. *Log Cabin,* 5 and 25 September 1840; 3 October 1840.
14. Greeley, *Recollections,* 166.
15. *New York Tribune,* 16 September 1842, 13 June 1843.
16. Ibid., 3 February 1844.
17. Ibid., 3 January 1846.
18. Roy M. Robbins, *Our Landed Heritage: The Public Domain, 1776–1970* (Lincoln: University of Nebraska Press, 1976), 171.
19. Roy M. Robbins, "Horace Greeley: Land Reform and Unemployment, 1837–1862," *Agricultural History* 7 (1933): 18–41.
20. Van Deusen, *Horace Greeley,* 61–63.

21. *New York Tribune,* 26 November 1845.
22. Ibid., 6 March 1847.
23. Ibid., 27 February 1847.
24. Ibid., 28 March 1848.
25. Ibid., 18 March 1845.
26. Greeley, *Recollections,* 217.
27. Greeley to Schuyler Colfax, 2 January 1848, Greeley Collection–New York.
28. Greeley, *Recollections,* 230.
29. *New York Tribune,* 28 March 1848.
30. Ibid., 25 March, 11 April 1850.
31. See especially the Greeley correspondence with Schuyler Colfax, Greeley Collection–New York.
32. *New York Tribune,* 26 December 1849, 27 June 1859.
33. Ibid., 4 July, 30 September 1850.
34. Ibid., 24 February 1851.
35. Ibid., 3 March 1851.
36. Robbins, *Our Landed Heritage,* 112.
37. *New York Tribune,* 24 January 1852.
38. Ibid., 14 April, 13, 18 March 1854.
39. Robins, *Our Landed Heritage,* 174–76.
40. *New York Tribune,* 2 February 1859.
41. Ibid., 5 February 1859.
42. Ibid.
43. Ibid., 2 March 1859.
44. Ibid., 30 January 1860.
45. Benjamin H. Hibbard, *A History of the Public Land Policies* (New York: Peter Smith, 1939), 378.
46. *New York Tribune,* 21 June 1860.
47. Ibid., 25, 30 June 1860.
48. Greeley to Colfax, 20 June 1860, Greeley Collection–New York.
49. Hibbard, *History of the Public Land,* 383.
50. *New York Tribune,* 25 August 1860.
51. Ibid., 5 December 1860.
52. Ibid., 1 February 1862.
53. Ibid., 21 March 1862.
54. Ibid., 7 May 1862.
55. Ibid., 6 June 1862; George M. Stephenson, *The Political History of the Public Lands from 1840 to 1862* (New York: Russell and Russell, 1917), 242–43, contains a good discussion on the passing of the Homestead Act.

56. Stephenson, *History of the Public Lands*, 243.
57. *New York Tribune*, 29 April 1867.
58. Ibid., 15 May 1867.
59. Everett Dick, *The Lure of the Land* (Lincoln: University of Nebraska Press, 1970), 157.
60. Fred A. Shannon, *The Farmer's Last Frontier: Agriculture 1860–1897* (New York: Farrar & Rinehart, 1945), 54.
61. Dick, *Lure of the Land*, 303.
62. Allan Nevins, *The War for the Union* (New York: Charles Scribner's Sons, 1960), ii: 204.

CHAPTER 4: BATTLING SLAVERY IN THE EXPANDING WEST

1. Greeley, *Recollections*, 64–65.
2. *New York Tribune*, 2 February 1843.
3. Ibid., 22 January 1845, 2 June 1845, 26 July 1845.
4. Ibid., 14 November 1842.
5. Ibid., 16 May 1843, 17 April 1844.
6. Ibid., 16 August 1845.
7. Ibid., 31 December 1845.
8. Ibid., 12 May 1846.
9. Ibid., 12 August 1846.
10. Ibid., 1 July 1846, 8 September 1847.
11. Ibid., 10 January 1854.
12. Greeley, *Recollections*, 292–93.
13. Allan Nevins, *A House Dividing: 1852–1857* (New York: Charles Scribner's Sons, 1947), 121.
14. *New York Tribune*, 1 February 1854.
15. Ibid.
16. Ibid., 25 October 1854.
17. Nevins, *House Dividing*, 307; Kenneth M. Stampp, *America in 1857: A Nation on the Brink* (New York: Oxford University Press, 1990), 145–46.
18. Nevins, *House Dividing*, 306.
19. 17 February 1855, quoted by Nevins, *House Dividing*, 381.
20. Ibid., 313–14.
21. *New York Tribune*, 19 January 1855.
22. Stampp, *America in 1857*, 4–5.
23. *New York Tribune*, 20 January 1855.
24. Ibid., 6 April, 22 May 1855.
25. Ibid., 17 April 1855.
26. Ibid., 12 December 1855, 4 March 1857.

27. Ibid., 20 January, 6 April 1855.
28. Ibid., 19 September 1855.
29. Greeley, *Recollections*, 294.
30. Greeley to Wm M. Chase, S. W. Peckham, and Wingate Hayes, 9 May 1856, Greeley Collection–New York.
31. Van Deusen, *Horace Greeley*, 183–85.
32. *New York Tribune*, 5 January 1857.
33. Allan Nevins, *The Emergence of Lincoln* (New York: Charles Scribner's Sons, 1950), 135.
34. Ibid., 229.
35. Stampp, *America in 1857*, 271.
36. *New York Tribune*, 29 October 1857; 16 November 1857.
37. William F. Zornow, *Kansas, A History of the Jayhawk State* (Norman: University of Oklahoma Press, 1957), 77–78; Stampp, *America in 1857*, 317–18.
38. Historians, including Allan Nevins, have long argued that Buchanan reversed his position on submitting the full constitution to the Kansas voters because he feared an offended South would secede. Kenneth Stampp rejects this reasoning and presents strong evidence that suggests that Buchanan acted not out of fear, but because his views coincided with those of the southerners in his cabinet. Stampp, *America in 1857*, 285.
39. *New York Tribune*, 19 December, 5 October, 20 November 1857.
40. Ibid., 19 January 1855.
41. Lincoln to Trumbull, 28 December 1857, Roy P. Basler, ed., *The Collected Works of Abraham Lincoln* (New Brunswick, N.J.: Rutgers University Press, 1953), 2:430.
42. *New York Tribune*, 12 November 1858.
43. Ibid.
44. Nevins, *Emergence of Lincoln*, 297.
45. Greeley to Colfax, 21 April 1858, Greeley Collection–New York.
46. Nevins, *Emergence of Lincoln*, 301.
47. Greeley, *Overland Journey*, 28–57; Zornow, *Kansas*, 80–81.

CHAPTER 5: FIGHTING FOR THE RAILROAD WEST

1. Greeley, *Recollections*, 360.
2. John Hoyt Williams, *A Great and Shining Road* (New York: Times Books, 1988), 16.
3. Ibid., 11.

4. Robert E. Riegel, *The Story of the Western Railroads: From 1852 through the Reign of the Giants* (Lincoln: University of Nebraska Press, 1926), 11.
5. *New York Tribune,* 8 March 1844.
6. Ibid., 11 September 1846.
7. Ibid.
8. Greeley, *Overland Journey,* 299–319.
9. Greeley, *Recollections,* 360.
10. Horace Greeley to John C. Underwood, 4 April 1862, Greeley Collection–Huntington.
11. Greeley, *Recollections,* 247; John F. Stover, *Iron Road to the West: American Railroads in the 1850s* (New York: Columbia University Press, 1978), 107.
12. *New York Tribune,* 11 May 1849.
13. Nevins, *House Dividing,* 85; Richard White, *"It's Your Misfortune and None of My Own"* (Norman: University of Oklahoma Press, 1991), 125.
14. *New York Tribune,* 22 January 1853.
15. Ibid., 28 January 1853.
16. Ibid., 18 August 1853, 26 January 1854.
17. Ibid., 24 May 1854.
18. Greeley to Colfax, 2 April 1853, Greeley Collection–New York.
19. *New York Tribune,* 15 June 1854, 28 November 1856, 13 January 1857, 5 July 1857.
20. Greeley to Colfax, 3 January 1857, Greeley Collection–New York.
21. *New York Tribune,* 5 July 1857; 1 January, 5 February 1859.
22. An attack of painful boils prevented him from returning overland.
23. Greeley, *Recollections,* 387.
24. Williams, *Great and Shining Road,* 39; George Kraus, *High Road to Promontory* (Palo Alto, Calif.: American West Publishing, 1969), 21.
25. Greeley, *Overland Journey,* 369–73.
26. Ibid., 374–76.
27. Ibid., 377.
28. Ibid., 374–79.
29. Ibid., 383–86.
30. Ibid., 386.
31. Ibid.
32. *New York Tribune,* 28 February 1840; 26 March, 17 April 1860.
33. Ibid., 7 May 1862.

34. LeRoy R. Hafen and Carl Coke Rister, *Western America* (New York: Prentice-Hall, 1950), 519; Robert V. Hine, *The American West* (Boston: Little, Brown, 1984), 159; Winther, *Transportation Frontier*, 99–100; Riegel, *Story of the Western Railroads*, 40–41.

35. Hafen and Rister, *Western America*, 521–25.

36. *New York Tribune*, 6 May 1871.

37. Ibid., 21 June 1871.

38. Ibid., 28 September 1871.

39. Ibid., 7 February 1871.

40. Ibid., 22 February, 4 March, 27 April, 4 October 1871.

41. Ibid., 6 March 1871.

42. Ibid., 29, 31 January, 7 March 1872; Van Deusen, *Horace Greeley*, 402–3.

43. Van Deusen, *Horace Greeley*, 404–5.

44. *New York Tribune*, 22 May 1872, letter dated 20 May 1872.

45. Winther, *Transportation Frontier*, 103–4; Hine, *American West*, 159–61; Riegel, *Story of the Western Railroads*, 41–43.

46. Riegel, *Story of the Western Railroads*, 46–47.

CHAPTER 6: SUPPORTING ASSOCIATION AND THE UNION COLONY

1. Greeley, *Overland Journey*, 208–18; Caroline Bengston, *Horace Greeley and the Founding of the Union Colony of Colorado* (Master's thesis, University of Chicago, 1910), 20; Rodman Paul, *The Far West and the Great Plains in Transition: 1859–1900* (New York: Harper & Row, 1988), 235; David Boyd, *A History: Greeley and the Union Colony of Colorado* (Dubuque, IA: Kendall Printing, 1987), 11–28; *New York Tribune*, 11, 15, 22, 25, 28 October, 13 November 1869.

2. Bengston, *Founding of the Union Colony*, 20; Boyd, *Greeley and the Union Colony*, 29–30, quotes a speech by Meeker recounting his conversation with Greeley.

3. Robert V. Hine, *Community on the American Frontier* (Norman: University of Oklahoma Press, 1980), 202.

4. Greeley, *Recollections*, 145.

5. Albert Brisbane, *Association* (New York: Greeley & McElrath, 1843), 3.

6. Ibid., 32; Edward K. Spann, *Brotherly Tomorrows: Movements for a Cooperative Society in America: 1820–1920* (New York: Columbia University Press, 1989), 69–70.

7. Horace Greeley, *Hints Toward Reforms* (New York: Harper & Brothers, 1850), 287–89.

8. Greeley to Griswold, 26 February 1841, Greeley Collection–Boston.

9. Greeley, *Hints Toward Reforms*, 291.
10. John Humphrey Noyes, *History of American Socialisms* (Philadelphia: J. B. Lippincott, 1870), 231–33.
11. Ralph Meeker, "The Founding of Greeley, Colorado," *Proceedings at the Unveiling of a Memorial to Horace Greeley at Chappaqua, N.Y., February 3, 1914* (Albany: University of the State of New York, 1915), 85.
12. Boyd, *Greeley and the Union Colony*, 16.
13. Noyes, *History of American Socialisms*, 562; Van Deusen, *Horace Greeley*, 79; *Tribune* and *Courier and Enquirer*, 20 November 1846–20 May 1847.
14. Greeley, *Recollections*, 147.
15. Ibid., 157.
16. Ibid., 149–50.
17. *New York Tribune*, 4 December 1869.
18. Ibid., 4 December 1869.
19. Ibid., 14 April 1871.
20. Ibid.
21. Ibid., 24 December 1869.
22. Ibid.
23. Ibid.; Greeley, *Overland Journey*, 145.
24. *New York Tribune*, 23 December 1869.
25. Ibid., 24 December 1869.
26. Horace Greeley to Nathan C. Meeker, 31 January 1870 and 19 February 1870, Greeley Collection, Denver Public Library (hereafter cited as Greeley Collection–Denver).
27. Horace Greeley to Nathan C. Meeker, 19 February 1870, Greeley Collection–Denver.
28. Bengston, *Founding of the Union Colony*, 35.
29. *New York Tribune*, 6 April 1870.
30. Ibid., 18 April 1870.
31. Bengston, *Founding of the Union Colony*, 36.
32. Henry T. West to Herbert Myrick, 2 June 1904, Greeley Collection–Huntington.
33. Ralph Meeker, *Horace Greeley and the Colony*, MS in the Greeley, Colorado Municipal Museum.
34. Horace Greeley to Nathan C. Meeker, 19 February 1870, Greeley Collection–Denver.
35. Van Deusen, *Horace Greeley*, 378.
36. Bengston, *Founding of the Union Colony*, 35.
37. *New York Tribune*, 11 January 1870.
38. Ibid., 24 March 1870.

39. *Daily Rocky Mountain News,* 13 October 1870.

40. Boyd, *Greeley and the Union Colony,* 83.

41. *Daily Colorado Tribune,* 15 October 1870.

42. *Daily Rocky Mountain News,* 11 November 1870.

43. Horace Greeley to Nathan C. Meeker, 19 February 1870, Greeley Collection–Denver.

44. Horace Greeley to Nathan C. Meeker, March 1871, Greeley Collection–Denver.

45. Horace Greeley to Nathan C. Meeker, 15 July 1871, Greeley Collection–Denver.

46. Boyd, *Greeley and the Union Colony,* 299.

47. Horace Greeley to Nathan C. Meeker, 11 March 1871, Greeley Collection–Denver.

48. Horace Greeley to Nathan C. Meeker, 9 June 1871, Greeley Collection–Denver.

49. Boyd, *Greeley and the Union Colony,* 299.

50. Horace Greeley to Nathan C. Meeker, 15 October 1872, Greeley Collection–Denver.

51. Horace Greeley to Nathan C. Meeker, 31 August 1870; Horace Greeley to Nathan C. Meeker, 5 November 1871, Greeley Collection–Denver.

52. Horace Greeley to Nathan C. Meeker, 18 March 1871, Greeley Collection–Denver.

53. Horace Greeley to Nathan C. Meeker, 25 August 1870, Greeley Collection–Denver.

54. Horace Greeley to Nathan C. Meeker, 3 October 1871, Greeley Collection–Denver.

55. Horace Greeley to Nathan C. Meeker, 10 October 1871, Greeley Collection–Denver.

56. Horace Greeley to Nathan C. Meeker, 12 November 1871, Greeley Collection–Denver.

57. Boyd, *Greeley and the Union Colony,* 305.

58. Delores Hayden, *Seven American Utopias* (Cambridge: MIT Press, 1976), 261.

59. Paul, *Far West and the Great Plains,* 236.

EPILOGUE

1. *New York Tribune,* 15 May 1872.

2. Greeley to Margaret Allen, 4 November 1872, Greeley Collection, Library of Congress.

BIBLIOGRAPHY

The New York Public Library possesses the largest collection of Greeley's correspondence and I am grateful that they made it available to me on microfilm. The Greeley Collections at Yale University and Boston Public Library are also available on microfilm. Karl Kabelac and his staff at the University of Rochester graciously assisted me in my search. The staff at the Manuscript Section of the Library of Congress not only aided me while I was there but also mailed me a copy of a document I had overlooked. The Huntington Library in San Marino, California, has several Greeley letters, and Virginia Renner, Head of the Reader Service, and her staff graciously made these available to me. Mr. Tom Dunnings, Head of the Manuscript Collection of the New York Historical Society, was very helpful during my research of the Greeley Collection there. Christian Brun and his staff in Special Collections at the University of California, Santa Barbara gave me innumerable hours of support and assistance. The staff of the Greeley (Colorado) Municipal Museum was especially helpful with material on the founding of Union Colony, as was Suzanne Schulze and the staff at the University of Northern Colorado in Greeley.

Primary Sources

Manuscripts

Greeley, Horace. Personal letters to friends. 1840 to 1871. Greeley Letters. Boston Public Library.

———. Personal letters to friends. 1839 to 1872. Greeley Letters. Library of Congress.

———. Personal letters to friends. 1845 to 1871. Greeley Letters. Huntington Library, San Marino, California.

———. Personal letters to and from friends. 1838 to 1865. Greeley Letters. New York Historical Society.

———. Personal letters to and from friends. 1838 to 1872. Greeley Letters. New York Public Library.

———. Personal letters to friends. 1838 to 1865. Greeley Papers. University of Rochester Library.

———. Personal letters to friends. 1841 to 1872. Horace Greeley Letters. Yale University Library.

Meeker, Ralph. "Horace Greeley and the Colony." Unpublished article in Greeley (Colorado) Municipal Museum.

Books, Articles, and Proceedings

Boyd, David. *A History: Greeley and The Union Colony of Colorado.* 1890. Reprint, Dubuque, IA: Kendall Printing, 1987.

Brooks, Noah. *Washington in Lincoln's Time.* Edited by Herbert Mitgang. New York: Rinehart, 1958.

Brockway, Beman. *Fifty Years of Journalism.* Watertown, N.Y.: Daily Times Printing and Publishing House, 1891.

Browning, Orville H. *The Diary of Orville Hickman Browning.* Edited by Theodore Calvin Pease and James G. Randall. Springfield: Illinois State Historical Library, 1927.

Central Pacific Railroad Company in Equitable Account with The United States, Growing out of the Issue of Subsidy Bonds in Aid of Construction: A review of the Testimony and Exhibits, The. New York: Henry Bessey, 1887.

Conway, Moncure D. *Autobiography Memories and Experiences of Moncure Daniel Conway.* Boston: Houghton Mifflin, 1904.

Greeley, Horace. *An American Conflict.* Hartford, Conn.: O. D. Case, 1879.

———. *Essays designed to elucidate the science of Political Economy.* Boston: Fields & Osgood, 1870.

———. "Greeley's Estimate of Lincoln." Reprint of Greeley's address of 1868. *Century Magazine,* July 1891.

———. *Hints Toward Reforms.* New York: Harper & Brothers, 1850.

———. *History of the Struggle for Slavery Extension or Restriction in the United States, from the Declaration of Independence to the Present Day. Mainly compiled and condensed from the journals of the Congress and other official records, and showing the vote by yeas and nays on the most important divisions in either house.* New York: Dix, Edwards, 1856.

———. *An Overland Journey: From New York to San Francisco in the Summer of 1859.* Edited by Charles T. Duncan. New York: Alfred A. Knopf, 1964.

Greeley, Horace, and John F. Cleveland. *A Political Text-book for 1860: Comprising a Brief View of Presidential Nominations and Elections including All the National Platforms ever yet Adopted: also, A History of the Struggle respecting Slavery in the Territories, and of the action of Congress as to the Freedom of the Public Lands, with the most notable speeches and letters of Messrs. Lincoln, Douglas, Bell, Cass, Seward, Everett, Breckenridge, H. V. Johnson, etc., etc., touching the questions of the day: and returns of all presidential elections since 1836.* New York: Tribune Association, 1860.

———. *Recollections of a Busy Life.* New York: J. B. Ford, 1868.

———. *What I Know of Farming.* New York: G. W. Carleton, 1871.

Lincoln, Abraham. *The Collected Works of Abraham Lincoln.* Edited by Roy P. Basler. New Brunswick, N.J.: Rutgers University Press, 1953.

Meeker, Ralph. "The Founding of Greeley, Colorado." In *Proceedings at the Unveiling of a Memorial to Horace Greeley at Chappaqua, N.Y. February 3, 1914.* Albany: University of the State of New York, 1915.

Richardson, Albert D. *Beyond the Mississippi.* Hartford, Conn: American Publishing, 1867.

Taylor, Bayard. *Eldorado, or Adventures in the Path of Empire.* New York: George P. Putnam, 1850.

Villard, Henry. *The Past and Present of the Pike's Peak Gold Regions.* Princeton, N.J.: Princeton University Press, 1932.

NEWSPAPERS

Boston Liberator
Chicago Tribune
New York Times
New York Tribune

SECONDARY SOURCES

Beecher, Jonathan. *Charles Fourier: The Visionary and His World.* Berkeley and Los Angeles: University of California Press, 1986.

Bengtson, Caroline. *Horace Greeley and the Founding of the Union Colony in Colorado.* Master's thesis, University of Chicago, 1910.

Bidwell, Percy W., and John I. Falconer. *History of Agriculture in the Northern United States, 1620–1860.* New York: Peter Smith, 1941.

Billington, Ray Allen. *America's Frontier Heritage.* San Francisco: Holt, Rinehart and Winston, 1966.

―――. *The Far Western Frontier, 1830–1860.* New York: Harper & Brothers, 1956.

―――. *Frederick Jackson Turner: Historian, Scholar, Teacher.* New York: Oxford University Press, 1973.

―――, ed. *The Frontier Thesis: A Valid Interpretation?* New York: Holt, Rinehart and Winston, 1966.

―――. *The Genesis of the Frontier Thesis.* San Marino, Calif.: Huntington Library, 1971.

Billington, Ray Allen, and Martin Ridge. *Westward Expansion.* New York: Macmillan, 1982.

Bogue, Allan G. *From Prairie to Corn Belt.* Chicago: University of Chicago Press, 1963.

Bremer, Robert H. *From the Depths: The Discovery of Poverty in the United States.* New York: New York University Press, 1956.

Brisbane, Albert. *Association.* New York: Greeley & McElrath, 1843.

―――. *Social Destiny of Man.* New York: Burt Franklin, 1840.

Carstensen, Vernon, ed. *The Public Lands: Studies in the History of the Public Domain.* Madison: University of Wisconsin Press, 1963.

Chamberlin, Everett. *The Struggle of '72.* Chicago: Union Publishing, 1872.

Clappe, Louise Amerial Knapp Smith. *The Shirley Letters.* Santa Barbara, Calif.: Peregrine Publishers, 1970.

Clark, William H. *Farms and Farmers.* Freeport, N.Y.: Books for Libraries Press, 1945.

Cleveland, Frederick A., and Fred Wilbur Powell. *Railroad Promotion and Capitalization in the United States.* New York: Longmans, Green, 1909.

Cochran, Thomas C. *Railroad Leaders, 1845–1890.* Cambridge: Harvard University Press, 1953.

Dale, Edward Everett. *Cow Country.* Norman: University of Oklahoma Press, 1942.

Dick, Everett. *The Lure of the Land.* Lincoln: University of Nebraska Press, 1970.

———. *The Sod-House Frontier: 1854–1890.* New York: D. Appleton-Century, 1937.

Edwards, Everett E., ed. *The Early Writings of Frederick Jackson Turner.* Madison: University of Wisconsin Press, 1938.

Erlich, John. *Sketch of the Life of Horace Greeley.* Chappaqua, N.Y.: Chappaqua Historical Society, 1911.

Fahrney, Ralph Ray. *Horace Greeley and the Tribune in the Civil War.* Cedar Rapids, Iowa: Torch Press, 1936.

Fite, Gilbert C. *The Farmers' Frontier, 1865–1900.* New York: Holt, Rinehart and Winston, 1966.

Galloway, John Debo. *The First Transcontinental Railroad.* New York: Simmons-Boardman, 1950.

Gates, Paul W. *The Farmer's Age: Agriculture, 1815–1860.* New York: Holt, Rinehart and Winston, 1960.

Gienapp, William E. *The Origins of the Republican Party, 1852–1856.* New York: Oxford University Press, 1987.

Hafen, LeRoy R., and Carl Coke Rister. *Western America.* New York: Prentice-Hall, 1950.

Hafen, LeRoy R., and Ann W. Hafen, eds. *Reports from Colorado: The Wildman Letters, 1859–1865.* Glendale, Calif.: Arthur H. Clark, 1961.

Hale, William Harlan. *Horace Greeley, Voice of the People.* New York: Harper & Brothers, 1950.

Hawgood, John A. *The Exploration and Settlement of the Trans-Mississippi West.* New York: Alfred A. Knopf, 1967.

Hill, Robert Tudor. *The Public Domain and Democracy.* New York: Columbia University Press, 1910.

Hinckley, Helen. *Rails from the West: A Biography of Theodore D. Judah.* San Marino, Calif.: Golden West Books, 1969.

Hine, Robert V. *Community on the American Frontier.* Norman: University of Oklahoma Press, 1980.

———. *The American West.* Boston: Little, Brown, 1984.

Holbrook, Stewart H. *The Story of American Railroads.* New York: Crown Publishers, 1947.

Horner, Harlan Hoyt. *Lincoln and Greeley.* Urbana: University of Illinois Press, 1953.

Isely, Jeter Allen. *Horace Greeley and the Republican Party, 1853–1861.* Princeton, N.J.: Princeton University Press, 1947.
Kluger, Richard. *The Paper: The Life and Death of the New York Herald Tribune.* New York: Alfred A. Knopf, 1985.
Kraus, George. *High Road to Promontory.* Palo Alto, Calif.: American West Publishing, 1969.
Lavender, David. *The Great West.* New York: Houghton Mifflin, 1965.
————. *Westward Vision: The Story of the Oregon Trail.* New York: McGraw-Hill, 1963.
Limerick, Patricia Nelson. *The Legacy of Conquest: The Unbroken Past of the American West.* New York: W. W. Norton, 1987.
Lund, Erik S. *Horace Greeley.* Boston: Twayne Publishers, 1981.
Monaghan, Jay. *The Overland Trail.* New York: Bobbs-Merrill, 1947.
Mott, Frank Luther. *American Journalism.* New York: Macmillan, 1950.
Nevins, Allan. *American Public Opinion.* Boston: Heath, 1928.
————. *The Emergence of Lincoln.* 2 vols. New York: Charles Scribner's Sons, 1950.
————. *Ordeal of the Union.* 2 vols. New York: Charles Scribner's Sons, 1947.
————. *The Origins of the Land-Grant Colleges and State Universities.* Washington D.C.: Civil War Centennial Commission, 1962.
Nordin, D. Sven. *Rich Harvest: A History of the Grange, 1867–1900.* Jackson: University Press of Mississippi, 1974.
Noyes, John Humphery. *History of American Socialisms.* Philadelphia: J. B. Lippincott, 1870.
Parke, Charles Ross. *Dreams to Dust: A Diary of the California Gold Rush, 1848–1850.* Edited by James E. Davis. Lincoln: University of Nebraska Press, 1989.
Parton, J[ames]. *The Life of Horace Greeley, Editor of the New York Tribune.* New York: Mason Brothers, 1855.
————. Revised edition. Boston: Fields & Osgood, 1869.
Paul, Rodman W. *California Gold: The Beginning of Mining in the Far West.* Lincoln: University of Nebraska Press, 1947.
————. *The Far West and the Great Plains in Transition: 1859–1900.* New York: Harper & Row, 1988.
Perkin, Robert L. *The First Hundred Years: An Informal History of Denver and the Rocky Mountain News.* Garden City, N.Y.: Doubleday, 1959.

Pillsbury, Albert E. "Memorial to Horace Greeley." In
  Proceedings and Commemorative Observances of 1911.
  Albany: University of the State of New York, 1911.
Potter, David M. *People of Plenty: Economic Abundance and the
  American Character.* Chicago: University of Chicago Press, 1954.
Riegel, Robert E. *The Story of the Western Railroads: From 1852
  through the Reign of the Giants.* Lincoln: University of
  Nebraska Press, 1926.
Robbins, Roy M. *Our Landed Heritage: The Public Domain,
  1776–1936.* Lincoln: University of Nebraska Press, 1962.
Sandburg, Carl. *Abraham Lincoln, The Prairie Years and the
  War Years.* New York: Dell Publishing, 1954.
Schmitt, Peter J. *Back to Nature: The Arcadian Myth in Urban
  America.* New York: Oxford University Press, 1969.
Seitz, Don C. *Horace Greeley, Founder of the New York Tribune.*
  1926. Reprint, New York: AMS Press, 1970.
Shannon, Fred A. *The Farmer's Last Frontier.* New York: Farrar
  & Rinehart, 1945.
Shenton, James P. *Robert John Walker: A Politician from Jackson to
  Lincoln.* New York: Columbia University Press, 1961.
Smith, Henry Nash. *Virgin Land: The American West as Symbol
  and Myth.* New York: Alfred A. Knopf, 1950.
Spann, Edward K. *Brotherly Tomorrows: Movements for a
  Cooperative Society in America: 1820–1920.* New York:
  Columbia University Press, 1989.
Spring, Leverett W. *Kansas, the Prelude to the War for the
  Union.* Boston: Houghton Mifflin, 1885.
Stampp, Kenneth M. *American in 1857.* New York: Oxford
  University Press, 1990.
Still, Bayard, ed. *The West: Contemporary Records of America's
  Expansion across the Continent: 1607–1890.* New York:
  Capricorn Books, 1961.
Stone, Irving. *They Also Ran: The Story of the Men Who Were
  Defeated for the Presidency.* New York: Doubleday, 1943.
Stover, John F. *Iron Road to the West: American Railroads in the
  1850s.* New York: Columbia University Press, 1978.
Taylor, Carl C. *The Farmers' Movement: 1620–1920.* New York:
  American Book, 1953.
Tebbel, John, and Sarah Miles Watts. *The Press and the
  Presidency.* New York: Oxford University Press, 1985.
Thomas, John L. *Alternative America.* Cambridge: Belknap
  Press, 1983.

Bibliography

Tibbles, Thomas Henry. *Buckskin and Blanket Days*. Lincoln: University of Nebraska Press, 1957.

Turner, Frederick Jackson. The Frontier in American History. New York: Henry Holt and Company, 1921.

———. *Rise of the New West, 1819–1829*. New York: Collier Books, 1962.

Unruh, John D., Jr. *The Plains Across: The Overland Emigrants and the Trans-Mississippi West, 1840–60*. Urbana: University of Illinois Press, 1982.

Utley, Robert M. *The Indian Frontier of the American West 1846–1890*. Albuquerque: University of New Mexico Press, 1984.

Van Deusen, Glyndon G. *Horace Greeley, Nineteenth-Century Crusader.* Philadelphia: University of Pennsylvania Press, 1953.

Wade, Richard C. *The Urban Frontier: The Rise of Western Cities, 1790–1830.* Cambridge: Harvard University Press, 1959.

Walker, Robert H. *Reform in America: The Continuing Frontier.* Lexington: University Press of Kentucky, 1985.

Webb, Walter Prescott. *The Great Plains.* Boston: Ginn Publishing, 1931.

White, Richard. *"It's Your Misfortune and None of My Own."* Norman: University of Oklahoma Press, 1991.

White, Morton, and Lucia White. *The Intellectual Versus the City: From Thomas Jefferson to Frank Lloyd Wright.* Cambridge: Harvard University Press, 1962.

Williams, John Hoyt. *A Great and Shining Road.* New York: Times Books, 1988.

Williams, Raymond. *The Country and the City.* London: Chatto & Windus, 1973.

Winther, Oscar Osburn. *The Transportation Frontier: Trans-Mississippi West 1865–1890.* New York: Holt, Rinehart and Winston, 1964.

Woods, Thomas A. *Knights of the Plow: Oliver H. Kelley and the Origins of the Grange in Republican Ideology.* Ames: Iowa State University Press, 1991.

Worster, Donald. *Rivers of Empire: Water, Aridity, and the Growth of the American West.* New York: Pantheon Books, 1985.

Zalerieskie, Francis Nicoll. *Horace Greeley the Editor.* New York: Funk and Wagnalls, 1890.

Zornow, William Frank. *Kansas: A History of the Jayhawk State.* Norman: University of Oklahoma Press, 1957.

INDEX

contributions to, 136; antislavery stance, 23–24, 72–73, 76; attributes, 135-36; Brown, John, 83; California, visits, 102; Carlyle's *Past and Present*, 56; Clay, Henry, admired and supported, 50, 54–55; Colorado, reports presence of gold in, 29; Congress, in, 25–26, 58; Davis, Jefferson, 12; death, 135; "deep plowing," 40; Department of Agriculture, 34, 44–45; farm at Chappaqua, 39; Fourierism, 116–20; free soil, contributions to, 137; Fremont, John C., 27; "Go West, young man," ix, 9; Grant, Ulysses S., 31–32; Greeley, Colorado, visits, 125–26; Homestead Law, contributions to, 137; influence and power, 14, 30; internal improvements, 22, 95; *Jeffersonian*, edits, 17–19, 51; Johnson, Andrew, 31; Kansas, supports free-soil immigration to, 80, 82, visits, 90; Kansas-Nebraska Bill, opposes, 24, 79–80, urges defeat of supporters of, 83; Land Grant College Act, 45–46, 50; Lecompton Constitution, 85–87; Lincoln, Abraham, 31; *Log Cabin*, edits, 19; Massachusetts Emigrant Aid Society, supports, 80; marries, 16; McElrath, forms partnership with, 20; Meeker, Nathaniel, 118, 127–29; Mexico, opposes war with, 74–75; National Reform Movement, 57–58; New York City, arrives, 4, 15; Oregon, opposes acquisition of, 11–12, 23, 73–74; overland journey to West, 29–30, 97, 101–2; Panic of 1837, financial plight following, 5, 17, 51; political alliance with Weed and Seward, 17, 24–25; presidential candidate, 32, 109-10, 134–35; protective tariff, supports, 54; "rain will follow the

plow," 42–43; Republican Party, 27–29, 84; River and Harbor Convention (1847), 96–97; safety valve theory, 4, 56; "scientific" methods on his farm, 37–38; Seward, William, 29; soil chemistry, 39–40; Texas, opposes statehood for, 74; Thoreau, Henry David, literary agent of, 7; transcontinental railroad, choice of routes, 98, 103–4, contributions to, 137-38, public financing for, 97, 104; trees, 42; *Tribune*, begins, 19–20; *Weekly Tribune*, begins, 20, resigns as editor to run for president, 32, 134, resumes editorship, 135; Union Colony, advice to, 119, 125, 127–28, contributions to, 129–30, treasurer of, 124; Weed, Thurlow, 17; *What I Know of Farming*, 39; Whitney, Asa, supports, 95; Wilmot Proviso, praises, 75.

Greeley, Mary Cheney "Molly" (wife), 16, 135

Greeley, Zack and Mary (parents), 14

Gregory's Diggings, Colorado gold mining camp, 29

Griswold, Rufus, 20, 26, 117

Grow, Galusha, 61, 62 (picture), 63, 69

Harrison, William Henry, 10, 19, 20, 55

History of the Struggle for Slavery Extension, A, 28

Houston, Sam, introduces homestead, 60

Jackson, Andrew, 16

Jefferson, Thomas, 7, 34, 135

Johnson, Andrew, 27, 31, 60, 63

Kansas-Nebraska Act, 24, 78–80

Land Grant College Act, 45–47

Lawrence, Amos A., 80

Lecompton Constitution, 85–89

Liberal Republicans, 32, 109, 134
Lincoln, Abraham: Bates, Edward,
   and, 31; in Congress, 27; elected
   president, 31; Homestead Act,
   and, 66–67; Morrill Land Grant
   College Act, and, 46; River and
   Harbor Convention 1847, attended,
   97; 1858 Senate race, and, 28–29,
   95; appoints Seward Secretary of
   State, 31; signs Transcontinental
   Railroad Bill, 106.

Massachusetts Emigrant Aid Society,
   80
McElrath, Thomas, 20
Meeker, Nathan, 114–30, 115
   (picture)
Meeker, Ralph, 124, 130
Missouri Compromise of 1820, 24, 78–
   79, 83, 87
Morrill, Justin S., 45–46

New Harmony, Indiana, 116, 136
Northern Pacific Company, 108–10

Osawatomie, Kansas Territory, 90
Overland Journey, An, 29, 101, 105
Owen, Robert Dale, 116, 136

Panic of 1837, 16, 36, 51, 61, 146
Pierce, Franklin, 79, 81
Political Textbook for 1860, A, 30
Polk, James K., 73–75, 97

Pottawatomie, Kansas Territory, 83
Preemption, 53–54, 64

Raymond, Henry J., 20, 27, 30, 119
River and Harbor Convention, 1847,
   97

Seward, William H., 17, 19, 24-28, 25
   (picture) 30–31, 57, 60, 73, 89
Soule, John, 136
Southern Pacific Railroad, 108

Taylor, Zachary, 75
Thayer, Eli, 80–81
Thoreau, Henry David, 7
Turner, Frederick Jackson, 4, 9, 12,
   86, 111, 139
Tyler, John, 10, 55, 74

Union Pacific Company, 106
Union Pacific Railroad, 111

Van Buren, Martin, 16

Washington, George, 7
Weed, Thurlow, 17, 18 (picture), 19,
   24–28, 30–31, 53, 57, 60, 73
What I Know of Farming, 39
Whitney, Asa, 94–95, 136
Wilmot Proviso, 75, 84

Young, Brigham, 30